Visual Reference Basics

Microsoft Office® 97

Diana Rain
Maria Reidelbach
Rosemary Shmavonian
Karl Schwartz

DDC Publishing

Acknowledgements

Managing Editor
Jennifer Frew

Project Managers
Jennifer Frew
Marni Ayers

English Editors
Marni Ayers
Aegina Berg

Technical Editors
Aegina Berg
Marni Ayers
Cathy Vessecky
Jennifer Frew

Layout and Design
Shawn Morningstar
Jeff Kurek
Karl Schwartz
Jeffrey A. Bates

Table of Contents

Excel

Access

PowerPoint

Outlook

Calendar

Contacts

Introduction

DDC's Visual Reference Basics series is designed to help you make the most of your Microsoft software. Newly updated to reflect changes and enhancements in the Microsoft Office 97 applications, the Visual Reference Basics are equally useful as instruction manuals or as desktop reference guides for the experienced user. With illustrations and clear explanations of every step involved, they make even complex processes easy to understand and follow.

The most distinctive feature of this series is its extensive use of visuals. Buttons, toolbars, screens and commands are all illustrated so that there is never any doubt that you are performing the right actions. Most information can be understood at a glance, without a lot of reading through dense and complicated instructions. With Visual Reference Basics, you learn what you need to know quickly and easily.

This book contains one hundred functions essential for optimal use of the Microsoft Office 97 suite applications. It covers approximately twenty functions per featured application (Word, Excel, Access, PowerPoint and Outlook), five basic Microsoft Office functions that pertain to all applications, and an Integration section that teaches and demonstrates how the different application can all work together.

Each section will cover the most commonly performed functions of the given application. Some functions will teach basic concepts while others will teach more advanced concepts. Therefore, it is recommended that you have a basic understanding of Windows and of each of the applications covered in this book.

The Visual Reference Basics series is an informative and convenient way to acquaint yourself with the capabilities of the Microsoft Office 97 suite package.

Office Basics

Because the Microsoft Office suite is several tools packaged together you will find that many of the functions work the same way. In Basics, several of the features common to Word, Excel, Access, PowerPoint, and Outlook are illustrated. As you become proficient in one Office application, you will find that those skills become applicable in the other applications as well.

Set Office Assistant Options

The Office Assistant is an automated and interactive helper that pops up onscreen when you perform certain actions. It is available in all Microsoft Office 97 applications and offers a variety of help options. Use the following procedures to set and control your Office Assistant.Use them also to choose a different Office Assistant character.

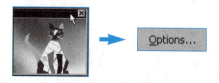

Notes:

• You can turn off all options so that the Office Assistant never starts automatically. To start the Office Assistant manually, click [?].

1 Click **Office Assistant** [?] to open the Office Assistant window if necessary.

2 Right-click in the Office Assistant window and click **Options** to display the Office Assistant dialog box.

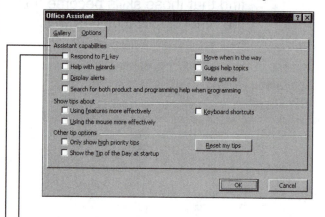

3 Set **Respond to F1 key** option:

Select the option if you want to start the Office Assistant when you press **F1**.

OR

Deselect the option if you want to open the Help Contents and Index when you press **F1**.

4 Select or deselect other **Assistant capabilities** options as follows:

• **Help with wizards**. Displays the Assistant when you select a command that starts a wizard. For example, importing an address book starts the Import Wizard.

• **Display alerts**. Displays general messages about actions. These are often troubleshooting tips.

• **Search for both product and programming help when programming**. Displays both Visual Basic and user help topics when you work in a Visual Basic module. If not selected, displays only programming help topics.

• **Move when in the way**. Shrinks the Assistant when you have not asked for help in five minutes and moves the Assistant window so that it is not on top of open dialog boxes.

• **Guess help topics**. Starts context-sensitive Assistant help. The Assistant tracks your actions and displays a list of help topics based on what you are doing when you ask for help. For example, if you have an appointment open when you click the Assistant to get help, the balloon lists a number of help topics on entering appointments.

• **Make sounds**. Enables or disables sound effects if you have a sound card.

5 Select or deselect **Show tips about** options to specify the kinds of tips you would like the Office Assistant to display.

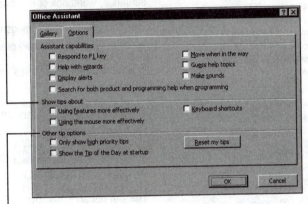

6 Select or deselect **Other tip options** to specify the kinds of tips you would like the Office Assistant to display:

Note: To view a tip, right-click the Assistant and click See **Tips**.

• **Only show high priority tips**. Deselect if the Assistant displays tips that are not useful.

• **Show the Tip of the Day at startup**. Displays an Outlook tip each time you start Outlook.

• **Reset my tips**. Outlook remembers which tips you have viewed and will not redisplay them. Click this button to start redisplaying tips that you have already seen.

7 To choose a different character, click the **Gallery** tab.

8 Click [OK].

Standard Toolbar and Formatting Toolbar

The Standard and Formatting toolbars are available in most Microsoft Office 97 applications. They are made up of buttons that quickly access various commonly performed tasks and throughout each of the applications.

Notes:

- To change the current toolbars, click View, Toolbars. A list of available toolbars for the current view is displayed. Click to select each toolbar you wish to display. You can also right-click any toolbar and select the toolbar you wish to display.

- To learn the name of a particular tool on any Microsoft toolbar, place your curser over a button. A ToolTip will appear providing the name of the button.

- The Standard toolbar in Outlook varies slightly from the one that is displayed in all other applications.

STANDARD TOOLBAR

1 The New button creates a new blank document, presentation, workbook or database.

2 The Open button brings you to the Open dialog box, which enables you to open previously created documents.

3 The Save button saves the current document with its current name.

4 The Print button prints current the document with all the default settings.

5 The Spell Check button checks for spelling errors throughout the document.

6 The Cut button moves selected information to Window's temporary clipboard to enable it to be moved to another location or document.

7 The Copy button copies the selected text or object to the Windows clipboard.

8 The Paste button pastes the current contents of the Windows clipboard at the blinking insertion point.

9 The Format Painter copies the formatting of selected text and applies it to other text.

10 The Undo button undoes the last action taken.

11 The Redo button redoes the last action that was undone. The drop-down button reveals a list of the actions that can be redone.

12 The Insert Hyperlink button is used to create interactive documents for the World Wide Web.

13 The Web toolbar button reveals a set of tools for working with the World Wide Web.

14 The Zoom button 41% controls the magnification of the slide. The number in the box represents the percentage of normal size at which the slide is displayed. Click on the drop-down list to see other magnification options.

15 The Help button accessed the Office Assistant and other help options.

FORMATTING TOOLBAR

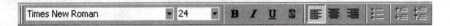

The Formatting Toolbar contains common commands that affect the appearance of text.The Formatting toolbar will vary significantly from application to application but the most common options are as followed:

1 The font drop-down list box Times New Roman assists in changing fonts quickly. Select the text to be affected and choose a font from the list.

2 The Font Size drop-down list 24 changes the size of text. Select the text to be affected and choose the correct size from the list. A size can also be typed in here.

3 **B** Bolds selected text.

4 *I* Italicizes selected text.

5 U Underlines selected text.

6 S Adds a shadow effect to selected text.

7 The alignment buttons set the position of selected within a document.

8 Creates a bulleted list.

9 Increases the spacing for selected paragraphs.

5

Save

Until a document has been saved to a disk, any changes that have been made to it exist only in the computer's temporary RAM. NOTE: With Outlook and Access, only the Save As option is available. Incremental tasks are saved to your hard drive as they are completed)

Notes:

- The keyboard shortcut for saving a document is Ctrl + S.

- New documents, as well as any changes made to an open document, are stored in the computer's temporary RAM (Random Access Memory) until the document, or changes to the document, are saved.

- If a power outage or system crash occurs, anything in RAM will be lost. To guard against such disaster, make it a habit to periodically save all open documents.

- A document's default name (Document 1, Document 2, etc.) can be changed when you save it for the first time.

1 Click **File**, **Save** to display the Save As dialog box.

OR

Click 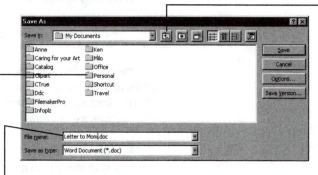.

2 In the **File name** text box, type desired name of file (your typing will replace the default name).

3 Double-click the folder in which you want to place the document.

4 Click **Up One Level** button to display the folders stored along with the folder currently displayed in the Save in text box.

- The first time you save a document, a Save As operation is performed by the computer This enables you to name the document for the first time and to indicate where you wish to save it. Each additional Save will simply save the most recent changes to the current document. The Save As dialog box will not reappear unless you choose Save As in place of Save.

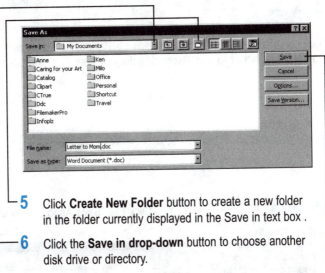

5 Click **Create New Folder** button to create a new folder in the folder currently displayed in the Save in text box .

6 Click the **Save in drop-down** button to choose another disk drive or directory.

7 Click **Save**. ──────────

7

Save As

The Save As command is used to save an additional copy of a document with a different name or to a different directory or disk than the original document.

Notes:

- If you give a document the same name as an existing document and try to save it to the same folder, it will replace the original document.

- After you use the Save As command, the document in the active window is the most recently named one.

1 Click **File**, **Save As** to display the Save As dialog box.

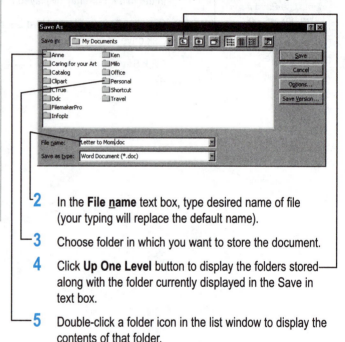

2 In the **File name** text box, type desired name of file (your typing will replace the default name).

3 Choose folder in which you want to store the document.

4 Click **Up One Level** button to display the folders stored along with the folder currently displayed in the Save in text box.

5 Double-click a folder icon in the list window to display the contents of that folder.

6 Click **Look in Favorites** button to display favorite folders that you have chosen.

7 Click **New Folder** button to create a new folder in the folder currently displayed in the Save in text box.

8 Click the **Save in** drop-down button to choose another disk drive.

9 Click **Save.**

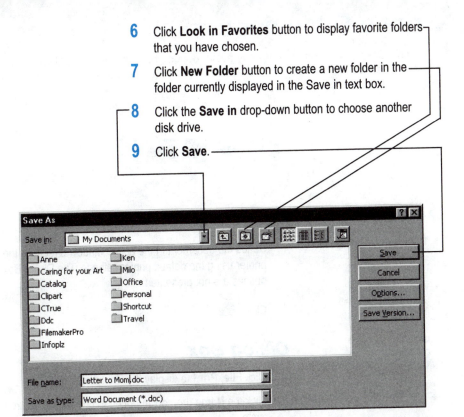

Print a Document

The Print command sends the currently active document to the printer. Until they are printed, print jobs are stored in Print Manager. The Print dialog box for each application may vary slightly.

Notes:

- The keyboard short-cut for printing a document is Ctrl + P.

- When documents are printing, a small icon appears on the Taskbar at the bottom right corner of the screen.

- What your actual printer button will say, depends on the type of printer you have, and what your printer name may be.

- Double-click the icon to open the printer dialog box. There you will see a list of pending print jobs, which you can rearrange or delete.

Toolbar

Sends the document in the active window directly to the printer using the default printer settings. The Dialog Box options are not presented.

1   Click 🖨 .

Dialog Box

1   Click **File**, **Print** to display the Print dialog box.

2   Click the **Name** drop down button to choose the desired printer.

3   Click the **Properties** button to change printer properties, such as print quality (options will vary depending on your printer).

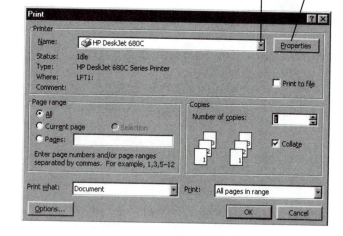

- You can print different page range combinations in a document. From the Print dialog box, click to select a page range:

  All to print all the pages of the document.

  Current page to print the page on which the insertion point is resting.

  Selection to print currently selected text and graphics (must have been selected before dialog box was opened).

  Pages to print desired page numbers (use a hyphen to specify a page range: 5-10; or use a comma to separate individual pages: 5,10).

- PowerPoint enables you to print slides, outlines, handouts or notes pages.

4 Check a desired **Page Range** to print (see options in note box to the right).

5 Click **Number of copies** and type the desired number of copies to print.

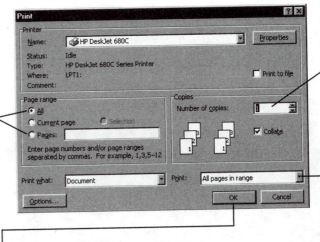

6 Click **Print** drop-down button to print odd or even pages only.

7 Click **OK**.

Word

Microsoft Office's word-processing application. Word is an extremely versatile program that allows you to create both visually exciting documents that can contain drawings, tables, charts, as well as basic correspondence and reports. This book will familiarize you with creating, formatting, and printing Word documents, as well as with various functions that will help you to get the most out of Word 97.

Arrange Windows

You can open several documents at once and layer or tile them. You can also open two windows within a document or split a document window and view two separate parts at once.

Window ➤ *Type Number of Document*

Notes:

- To show all windows on the desktop, right-click the taskbar background and click Tile Horizontally or Tile Vertically.

- Change the setting on the General tab of the Options dialog to display your text in white on a blue background.

Bring a Window to the Front

Click on any visible part of the window.

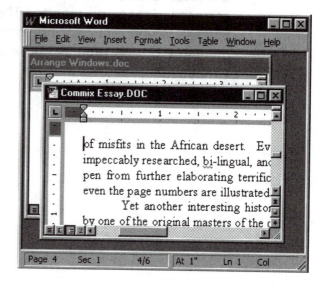

OR

1 Click **Window**.

2 Click desired document name at bottom part of menu, or press document number on the keyboard.

Notes:

- Use the document control buttons in the upper right corner to do the following actions to a window:

   Minimize

  Maximize

  Restore

  Close

Tile Windows Horizontally

1 Click **Window, Arrange All**.

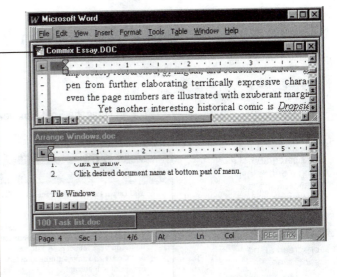

2 The title bar of the active document is displayed in the brighter color.

Notes:

* Splitting windows enables you to view two separate sections of a document simultaneously. For example, you may need to compare information in the first paragraph of a long report with information in the last paragraph. Splitting the document window enables you to view both sections onscreen at the same time.

Split Document Window

1   Click and drag the **Split Box** down to the desired new location.

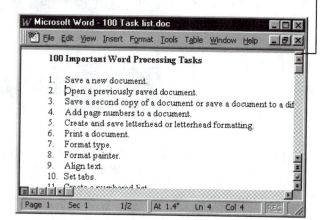

2   Each pane will have its own scroll buttons.

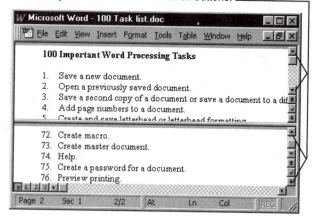

Open Another Window on a Document

1 Click **Window**, **New Window** to open another window within the same document.

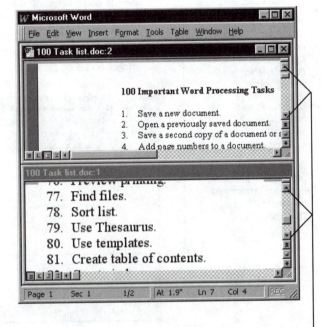

2 Each window will have its own scroll buttons, and the document can also be seen in different View types. Editing to information in either window will be saved to the same file.

Move Around within a Document

Most documents are too big to be viewed in the window in their entirety. Here's how to get around your document quickly.

1 Use the Scroll bar buttons to move to where you desire:
- the end of the document
- the beginning of the document
- a specific part of the document (click and drag the square)

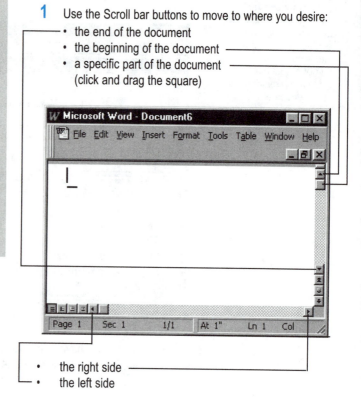

- the right side
- the left side

Notes:

• Once an object is selected, you can use the next and previous page arrows to move from object to object.

• the previous page
• the next page

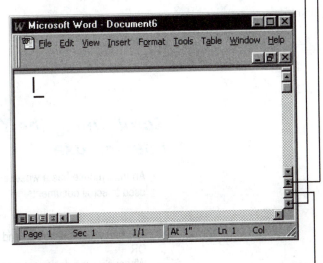

• Select **Browse Object** and then:

→ Go to a particular page number (see **Go To**)

🔍 Find text (see **Find Text**)

✏️ Browse by edits (see **Track Changes**)

Browse by heading (see **Outline** and **Styles**)

🖼️ Browse by graphic

Browse by table

{a} Browse by field (see **Forms**)

Browse by Endnote

Browse by Footnote

Browse by Comment

Browse by Section

Browse by Page

Scroll Using the Wheel on the Intellimouse

An Intellimouse has a wheel in the middle that can be used to scroll documents.

1 Roll the wheel to scroll up and down in the document
OR
Wheel-click the document window to change the vertical scroll bar.

2 Point above or below the center divider to scroll up or down in the document. The further you point from the center, the faster you scroll.

3 Wheel-click to go back to normal scrolling.

Continue

Templates

Templates are special documents containing formatting and text that can be used as the basis for other documents.

Create a New Document Based on a Template

1 Click **File**, **New** to open the Templates dialog box.

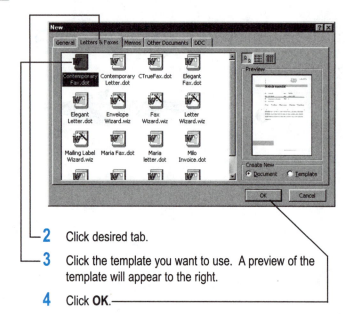

2 Click desired tab.

3 Click the template you want to use. A preview of the template will appear to the right.

4 Click **OK**.

Notes:

- There are more templates available on the Word 97 or Office 97 CD-ROM. They can be located in the ValuPack, Templates folder.

Create a New Template

1 Click **File**, **New** to open the Templates dialog box.

2 Click desired tab.

3 Click template to use as base template.

4 Click **Template** option button.

5 Click **OK**.

6 Customize the template as desired.

7 Click Save button ⊟.

Name the template, making sure to retain the "dot" extension. Save the template in desired folder within the Templates folder.

Align Text

Text can be aligned at the left or right margins, evenly justified between margins, or centered along a vertical axis.

Notes:

- The keyboard shortcuts for aligning text are:

    Left: Ctrl + L

    Right: Ctrl + R

    Justified: Ctrl + J

    Centered: Ctrl + E

Toolbar

1 Click and drag over text to format.
OR
Point to and click the spot where you plan to type new text.

2 Click desired toolbar button:

   • **Left align** button ▤

   • **Right align** button ▤

   • **Justify** (left and right align) button ▤

   • **Center align** button ▤

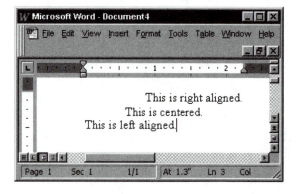

- To align text more than one way on a single line, use tabs.

- To make lines closer to the same length (less ragged), change the hyphenation zone.

Dialog Box

1 Click and drag over text to format.
OR
Point to and click the spot where you plan to type new text.

2 Click **Format**, **Paragraph** to display the Paragraph dialog box.

3 Click the **Indents and Spacing** tab.

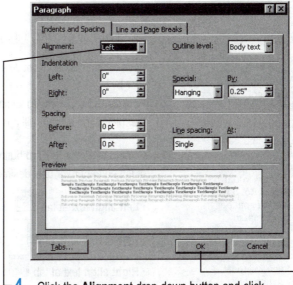

4 Click the **Alignment** drop-down button and click desired alignment.

5 Click **OK**

Tabs

Use tabs to align text precisely on the page. Tabs can be used to left align, center align, right align, or decimal align text.

Notes:

- Tab settings can be placed using the ruler, or by accessing the Tabs dialog box additional options. (If ruler is not visible, click View, Rule.)

- Because word processor applications do not read space markings in the same way that typewriters do, do not use the space bar to attempt to align text or objects on a page. What looks aligned onscreen will most likely not print the same way. Always use tabs and indent markers to align your document. Be sure to double check the final outcome in Print Preview.

- To align text more than one way on a single line, use tabs.

- To make lines closer to the same length (less ragged), change the hyphenation zone.

Ruler

1 Click and drag over text to be affected by tab sets.
OR
Point to and click the spot where you plan to type and tab new text.

2 Point to and click desired location on the bottom edge of the ruler. A tab symbol will appear.

3 Point to and click the **Tab** button at left edge of ruler until desired tab appears:

- **Left align** text at tab

- **Center** text on tab

- **Right align** text at tab

- **Decimal align** text at tab

4 To move a tab, click and drag its symbol to a new location on the ruler.

5 To remove a tab, click and drag its symbol off the ruler.

- To create regularly-spaced tabs, in the Tabs dialog box enter a distance in the Default Tab Stops text field.

- To insert a tab in a table, press Ctrl + Tab.

- A leader is a row of dots or a line extending the width of the tab. It is often used in tables of contents.

Dialog Box

1 Click and drag over text to be affected by tab sets.
OR
Point and click to the spot where you plan to type and tab new text.

2 Click **Format**, **Tabs** to display the Tabs dialog box.

3 Type the desired tab location in the **Tab stop position** text box (the default tab alignment is relative to the left margin).

4 Click the desired **Alignment** radio button.

5 Click the desired **Leader** radio button.

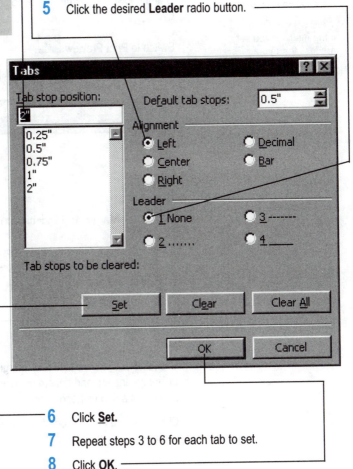

6 Click **Set**.

7 Repeat steps 3 to 6 for each tab to set.

8 Click **OK**.

Margin Settings

Page margins can be quickly changed using the ruler or they can be set to precise locations by using the dialog box.

Ruler

1 If necessary, switch to Page Layout view  (the button is at the lower left corner of the document window)

OR

Switch to Print Preview .

2 If necessary, click **View**, **Ruler** to display the rulers.

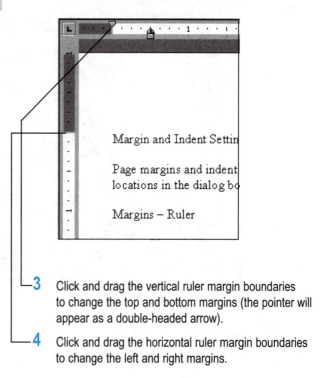

3 Click and drag the vertical ruler margin boundaries to change the top and bottom margins (the pointer will appear as a double-headed arrow).

4 Click and drag the horizontal ruler margin boundaries to change the left and right margins.

Notes:

- With some specialized layouts (such as labels), you will get a warning that the page margins are too wide. Try ignoring the warning and printing your layout (sometimes the overage is blank area and to fix it would misalign the labels).

Dialog Box

1 If necessary, select section of text for which you want to change margins.

2 Click **File**, **Page Setup**, **Margins** to view the Margins tab of the Page Setup dialog box.

3 Type desired margin width in the appropriate **Margins** text boxes (a preview will appear to the right).

4 Type desired **Header and Footer** margins in the **From Edge** text boxes.

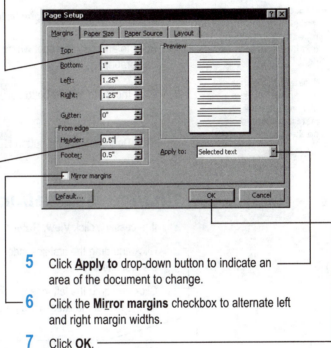

5 Click **Apply to** drop-down button to indicate an area of the document to change.

6 Click the **Mirror margins** checkbox to alternate left and right margin widths.

7 Click **OK**.

Indent Paragraphs

Paragraphs can be quickly indented from the left using the toolbar buttons. Using the Paragraph dialog box, you can also set paragraphs with only the first line indented or with all lines following the first indentation (a hanging indent).

Format ➡ ▤ Paragraph... ➡ Indents and Spacing

Notes:

- Click the Increase Indent button repeatedly to move text further to the right.

- A paragraph with a hanging indent has all lines after the first line indented on the left.

Toolbar

1 Click and drag over paragraphs to indent
OR
Point to and click the spot where you plan to type new paragraphs.

2 Click **Increase Indent** button to move text to the right
OR

Click **Decrease Indent** button to move text to the left.

Change Indentation Spacing

1 If necessary, click **View**, **Ruler** to display the ruler.

2 Click and drag the first line indent marker to change the first line of text.

3 Click and drag the left indent marker to change the indent for the rest of the lines in the paragraph.

It's a funny time in the history of comic books -- seriously. Since their invention in 1935 they've

4 Click and drag the left indent box to change the indent for all lines of text.

5 Click and drag the right indent box to change the right indent.

30

Dialog Box

1   Click and drag over paragraphs to indent.
OR
Point to and click the spot where you plan to type new paragraphs.

2   Click **Format**, **Paragraph** to display the Paragraph dialog box.

3   If necessary, click the **Indents and Spacing** tab to bring it to the front.

4   Click the **Left** text box and type desired distance to indent from the left margin.

5   Click **Right** text box and type the desired distance to indent from the right margin.

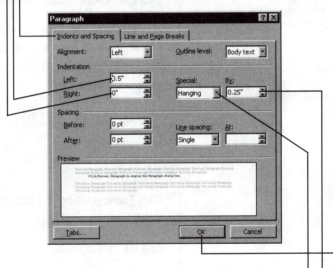

6   Click the **Special** drop-down button and click the desired indent type.

7   Click the **By** text box and type distance for special indenting from the left margin.

8   Click **OK**.

Spelling

Word automatically checks the spelling of the words in your document and underlines those it does not recognize with a wavy red line.

1 Right-click the misspelled word.

2 From the list of possible spelling choices, click desired spelling
OR
click **Ignore All** to accept the word throughout the document
OR
click **Add** to add the word to Word's dictionary. This will prevent the word from being specified as misspelled in all future documents.

Toolbar

Click the spelling button 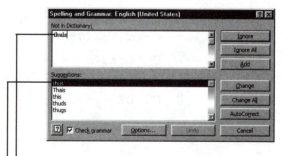 to bring up the Spelling and Grammar dialog box.

Dialog box

1 Click **Tools**, **Spelling and Grammar** to open the Spelling dialog box
OR
click the Spelling button.

2 The first misspelled word will appear in the
Not in Dictionary text box. You can do one of the following:
- Click the correctly spelled word in the **Suggestions** list and click **Change**.
- Click the correctly spelled word in the Suggestions list and click **Change All** to correct all identical misspellings throughout the document.

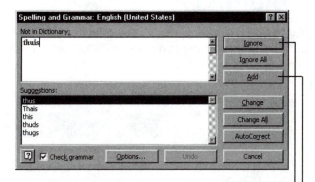

- Click the correctly spelled word in the **Suggestions** list and click **AutoCorrect** to automatically correct the identical misspelling when you type it in the future.
- Click **Ignore** to leave the word as it is and go on to the next word.
- Click **Add** to add the word to the dictionary for future spell checks.

3 Repeat step 2 until all words are checked.

4 Click **OK** to close the Spelling and Grammar dialog box.

Columns

The Columns feature can be used to format any number and size of columns, depending on the width of your paper. You can create columns by using the toolbar and ruler, or by using the dialog box.

Notes:

- To create columns with items that align horizontally, create a table.

- To add vertical lines between columns, click the checkbox in the Columns dialog box. To see the lines, view your document in Page Layout View or Print Preview.

Toolbar

Click and hold Columns button [image], then drag across number of columns desired.

Dialog Box

1 Point to and click where you want to start typing text in columns.
OR
Select text to be formatted in columns.

2 Click **Format**, **Columns** to open the Columns dialog box.

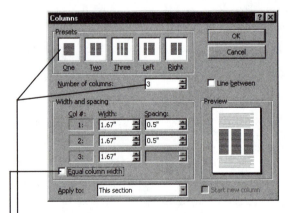

3 Click desired number of columns in the **Presets** area.
OR
Click **Number of columns** text box and type desired number.

4 Check or clear **Equal column width** box, as desired.

5 Change column **Width**, as desired.

6 Change **Spacing** between columns, as desired.

7 Click **OK** when you are finished.

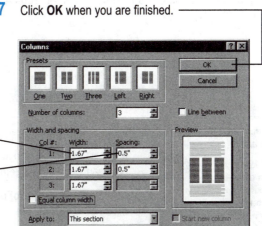

Change Column Width and Spacing

Column spacing can be easily changed by either using the ruler or accessing the Columns dialog box.

1 If necessary, click **View**, **Ruler** to display the ruler.

2 Click and drag edges of columns to change column width or spacing.

3 Change indents as with regular text

Start a New Column

Use a Column Break to begin typing at the top of a new column.

1 Click **Insert**, **Break** to open the Break dialog box.

2 Click **Column break** button.

3 Click **OK**.

35

Tables: Create and Edit a Table

Tables are useful to arrange text or numbers in column or row format. Tables can be formatted with a variety of border and shading styles. You can add or remove rows and columns from a table at any time.

Notes:

- To create newspaper style columns, use the Columns feature.

- To include a section of an Excel spreadsheet in your document use the Embed and Link features.

Create a Simple Table

1 On the Standard toolbar, click the Insert Table button and drag over desired number of columns and rows (you can also add and remove columns and rows later).

2 Click **Table**, **Table AutoFormat** to open the AutoFormat dialog box.

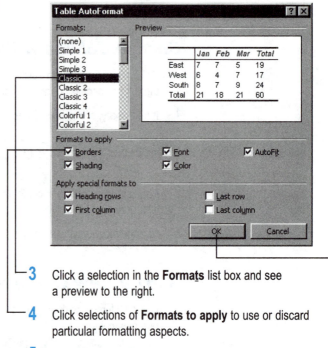

3 Click a selection in the **Formats** list box and see a preview to the right.

4 Click selections of **Formats to apply** to use or discard particular formatting aspects.

5 Click **OK**.

6 To add information to the table, point and click the first cell.

7 Type information, then press **Tab** to move to next cell.

Create a Complicated or Irregular Table

1 On the standard toolbar, click the Tables and Borders

button 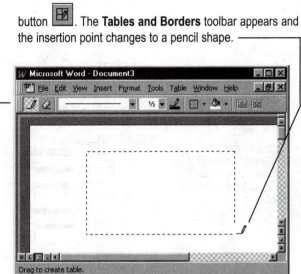. The **Tables and Borders** toolbar appears and the insertion point changes to a pencil shape.

2 Click and drag to draw a rectangle the size of the entire table.

3 Click and drag to draw columns and rows inside the table.

4 To erase a line, click the Eraser button and drag over line to remove.

5 To add more lines, click the Draw Table button.

6 To add information to the table, point and click first cell.

7 Type information, then press **Tab** to move to next cell.

Tables: Create and Edit a Table

continued . . .

Notes:

- To apply formats or edits to a whole table, click Table, Select Table.

- To display the Table and Borders toolbar, right-click any toolbar and click Tables and Borders.

Insert a Column

1 Point to and click the area just above the table where you want to add the columns.

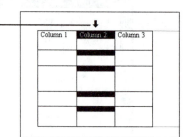

2 Click the Insert Columns button ![button]. (The button becomes visible once the column is selected.) The original columns will shift to the right to accommodate the new column.

Insert Row

1 Point to and click or click and drag in the area just left of the table where you want to add the rows.

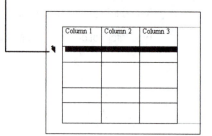

2 Click the Insert Rows button ![button]. (The button becomes visible once the column is selected.) The original rows will shift down to accommodate the new row.

Remove Rows or Columns

1   Click and drag area to left of rows or above columns to remove.

2   Click **Table**, **Delete Rows** or **Delete Columns**.

Split Cells

1   Click and drag to select cells to split.

2   On the Tables and Borders toolbar, click the Split Cells

button 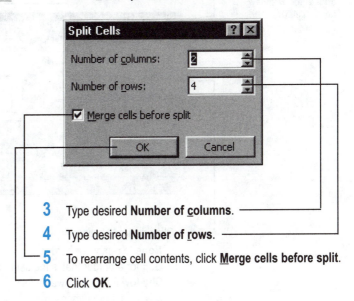 to open the Split Cells dialog box
OR
click **Table**, **Split Cells**.

3   Type desired **Number of columns**.

4   Type desired **Number of rows**.

5   To rearrange cell contents, click **Merge cells before split**.

6   Click **OK**.

Merge Cells

1   Click and drag over cells to merge.

2   On the Tables and Borders toolbar, click the Merge

Cells button
OR
Click **Table**, **Merge Cells**.

Borders: Create Borders for Pages and Paragraphs

Your pages and paragraphs can be bordered by a variety of lines, colors and shapes.

Format ➡ Borders and Shading... ➡ Page Border

Notes:

- To change each border separately, click desired line style and–in the Preview area–click the border to change.

1 Click **Format**, **Borders and Shading** to open the Borders and Shading dialog box.

2 Click the **Page Border** tab to bring it to the front.

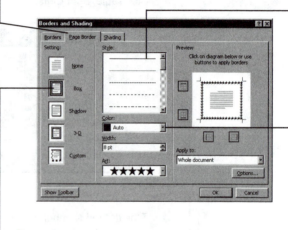

3 Click desired Setting:
- **None** to remove a border
- **Box** for a border that is the same on all sides
- **Shadow** for a shadowed effect
- **3-D** for a three dimensional effect
- **Custom** to choose different borders for different sides.

4 In the **Style** list box, click desired border style (check the Preview to the right to see the effect you've created).

5 Click the **Color** drop-down button to choose a color for the border.

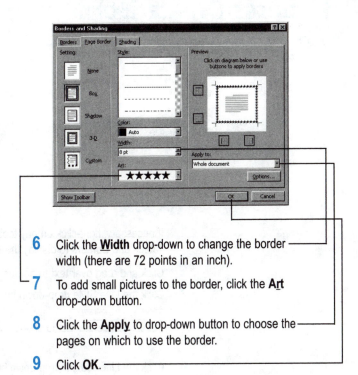

6 Click the **Width** drop-down to change the border width (there are 72 points in an inch).

7 To add small pictures to the border, click the **Art** drop-down button.

8 Click the **Apply** to drop-down button to choose the pages on which to use the border.

9 Click **OK**.

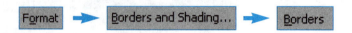

Toolbar

1 If necessary, right-click on any toolbar area and click Tables and Borders to display the toolbar.

2 Click and drag over text to border.

3 Click the Line Style drop-down button

to choose desired line style.

4 Click the Line Weight drop-down button to choose desired line weight.

5 Click the Border Color button to click desired line color.

6 Click the Borders drop-down button to choose which sides to border.

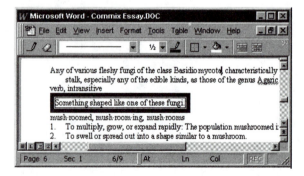

Dialog Box

1 Click **Format**, **Borders and Shading** to open the Borders and Shading dialog box.

2 Click the **Borders** tab to bring it to the front.

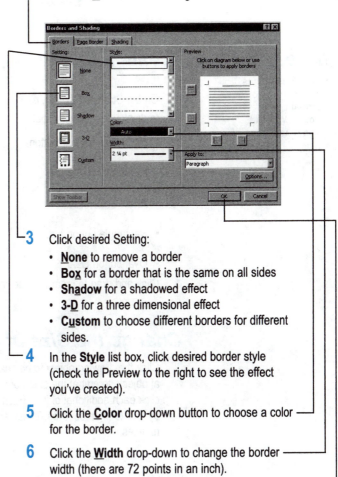

3 Click desired Setting:
- **None** to remove a border
- **Box** for a border that is the same on all sides
- **Shadow** for a shadowed effect
- **3-D** for a three dimensional effect
- **Custom** to choose different borders for different sides.

4 In the **Style** list box, click desired border style (check the Preview to the right to see the effect you've created).

5 Click the **Color** drop-down button to choose a color for the border.

6 Click the **Width** drop-down to change the border width (there are 72 points in an inch).

7 Click **OK**.

Drawing

The Drawing feature allows you to create your own drawing or edit a pre-existing drawing.

Create a Shape

1 On the Standard toolbar, click the Drawing button to display the Drawing toolbar.

2 Click desired toolbar button:

• Line button ⟍

• Arrow button ↘

• Rectangle button ▢

• Oval button ⬭

3 Click and drag to create the desired shape.

Change the Size of a Drawing

1 Click the drawing object to be changed. To select additional objects to edit at the same time, hold the Shift key and click each additional object. Each object will be surrounded by four to eight squares. These squares are referred to as handles.

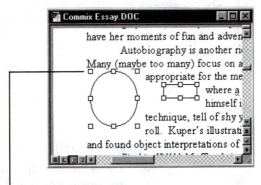

2 To change the size of selected objects, point to a handle (the pointer will appear as a two-headed arrow) and drag the handle out or in.

Move a Drawing

1 Click the drawing object to be moved. To select additional objects to move at the same time, hold the Shift key and click each additional object.

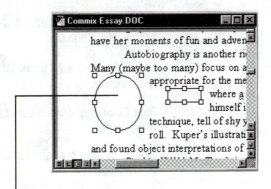

2 To move selected objects, point to an area within the area surrounded by the handles (the pointer will appear as a four-headed arrow), then click and drag the objects to the desired new location.

Change Appearance of Drawing

Note: Outline, fill, and other aspects can be changed depending on the type of drawing you are editing.

1 On the Standard toolbar, click the Drawing button to display the **Drawing toolbar.**

2 Click the drawing object to be changed. To select additional objects to edit at the same time, hold the Shift key and click each additional object.

3 Click the following toolbar buttons to use access certain effects:

- **Fill Color** drop-down button to change the interior color of the drawing.

- **Line Color** drop-down button to change the color of the outline.

- **Font Color** drop-down button to change the color of interior text.

- **Line Style** drop-down to change the width and style of outline.

- **Dash Style** drop-down to choose a dashed outline.

- **Shadow** drop-down to choose a shadow.

- **3-D** drop-down to choose a three-dimensional effect.

Rotate Drawing

1 On the standard toolbar, click the Drawing button to display the **Drawing toolbar.**

2 Click drawing object to rotate. To select additional objects to rotate at the same time, hold the Shift key and click each additional object.

3 Click the Free Rotate button 　. The handles at the corners become circles and the pointer changes to a rotation symbol.

4 Click and drag a handle until drawing is rotated as desired.

Flip Drawing

1 On the standard toolbar, click the Drawing button 　 to display the **Drawing toolbar.**

2 Click drawing object to change. To select additional objects to edit at the same time, hold the **Shift** key and click each additional object.

3 Click the Draw drop-down button 　.

4 Click **Rotate** or **Flip,** then click desired new position.

Group Drawings

Several drawing objects can be combined into one object to make editing easier.

1 On the Standard toolbar, click the Drawing button 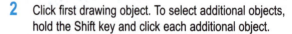 to display the **Drawing toolbar.**

2 Click first drawing object. To select additional objects, hold the Shift key and click each additional object.

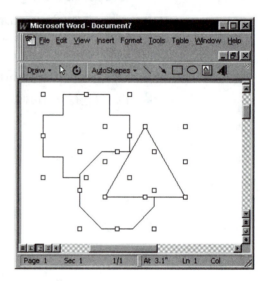

3 Click the Draw drop-down button [Draw ▾]
OR
right-click the shapes and click **Grouping**.

4 Click **Group**. The objects will have only one set of handles.

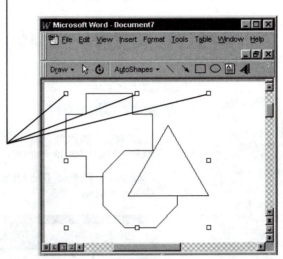

Change Object Overlap

1 On the Standard toolbar, click the Drawing button to display the **Drawing toolbar**.

2 Click first object.

3 Click the Draw drop-down button [Draw ▾]
OR
right-click object.

4 Click **Order**, then click desired position of object.

Pictures: Insert and Edit Clip Art and Pictures

There are many ways of including images in your documents.
(See also Drawing and AutoShape)

Notes:

- Click the Import Clips button in the Clip Gallery window to add clip art to the gallery.

- Click the Find button in the Clip Gallery window to search for the art based on key words.

- Click the Pictures, Sounds or Videos tabs to add other types of clips to your documents.

Insert Clip Art

Insert an image from Word's clip art collection, or from a clip art collection of your own.

1   Click **Insert**, **Picture**, **Clip Art** to open the Clip Gallery window.

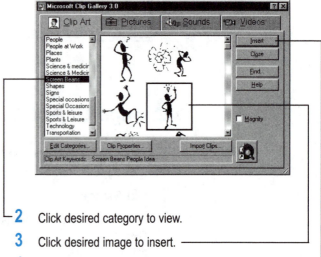

2   Click desired category to view.

3   Click desired image to insert.

4   Click **Insert** (see below to size and position the image).

Insert Picture

Inserts an image saved to a separate file.

1   Click **Insert**, **Picture**, **From File** to open the Insert Picture dialog box.

2   Select desired file name

3   Click **Insert** (see below to size and position the image).

Change Image Size

1   If necessary, click picture to select it.

2   Click and drag one of the picture's handles to the desired size

AutoShapes

AutoShapes is a collection of shapes and drawings–such as banners, arrows and callouts–which can be inserted into documents and customized.

Notes:

- Add colors, shadows and 3-D effects to the AutoShape by using the Drawing toolbar.

- To display the Drawing toolbar, right click on any toolbar and click Drawing.

1 Click **Insert**, **Picture**, **AutoShapes** to display the AutoShapes and Drawing toolbars.

2 Click desired shape to draw, then choose a specific shape:

- Lines

- Basic Shapes

- Block Arrows

- Flowchart

- Stars and Banners

- Callouts

3 Click and drag on document page to draw the AutoShape (for curvy lines, double-click when finished).

4 To make shape smaller or larger, click and drag a handle.

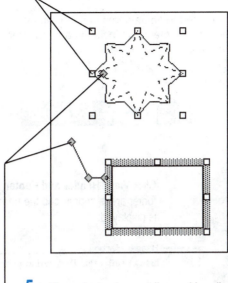

5 Many shapes have a diamond handle to click and drag to change specific proportions of the AutoShape (to make stars pointier, for instance, or to change the stem of a callout).

6 Return to the document window by clicking outside the AutoShape.

Headers and Footers

Headers and footers are used to contain text that will repeat at the top or bottom of consecutive pages. Headers and footers can include page numbers, dates, filenames, and other specialized information.

1 Click **View**, **Header and Footer**. The header and footer areas appear and the header and footer toolbar is displayed.

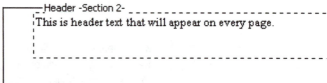

Header -Section 2-

This is header text that will appear on every page.

2 Type text to repeat in the header or footer area defined by the dotted line. Use the toolbar buttons to include special information where desired:

- Page number button [#]

- Number of pages button [⊡]

- Format page number button [⊡]

- Date button [⊡]

- Time button [⊘]

3 When finished, click [Close] .

Change Header or Footer

1 View the page where you want the new header or footer to begin to appear.

2 Insert a section break by clicking **Insert**, **Break** and choosing desired break (see **Section Breaks**).

3 If necessary, click **View**, **Header and Footer** to display the header and footer areas.

4 On the header and footer toolbar, click [icon].

5 Type the desired new header or footer.

Edit Header or Footer

1 If necessary, click **View**, **Header and Footer** to display the header and footer areas.

2 Click in header or footer area and edit text as desired.

3 Click **Close**.

Macros

A Macro is a recording of text and commands that can then be played back. Use macros to automate repetitive tasks.

Notes:

- It's handy to create a macro that opens your favorite template and assign the macro to a toolbar button.

- If, while you're recording a macro, you need to perform actions you don't want to record, click the Pause button. Click Pause again to restart recording.

- Do not use spaces in the Macro name. Word will not be able to recognize them.

Record Macro

1 Click **Tools**, **Macro**, **Record New Macro** to open the Record Macro dialog box.

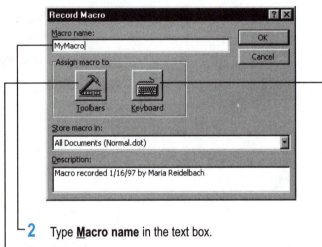

2 Type **Macro name** in the text box.

3 To add a toolbar button that will run the macro, click **Toolbars**.

4 In the **Commands** list box that appears, click and drag the new macro name to the desired spot on the toolbar.

5 To assign a keyboard shortcut that will run the macro, click **Keyboard**.

6 Type key combination (usually using the Ctrl or Alt keys in combination with letters or numbers) in the **Press new shortcut** key text box. If the key combination you type is currently used by another command, that command will appear below.

7 Click **Assign** when finished.

8 Click **Close** to return to the document window. The macro toolbar is displayed.

9 Perform the actions that you wish to record.

10 When finished, click the Stop Recording button 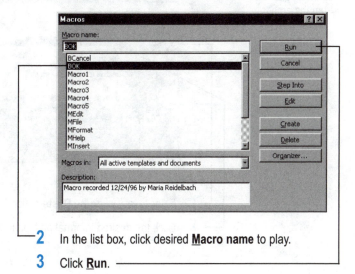 on the Macro toolbar.

Play Macro

If you assigned your macro to a toolbar button or a shortcut key sequence, it can be played back by accessing that button or key combination. It may also be played back by doing the following:

1 Click **Tools**, **Macro**, **Macros** to open the Macro dialog box.

2 In the list box, click desired **Macro name** to play.

3 Click **Run**.

Embed and Link Objects

The Embed feature is used to add information from a file created in another program to a Word file. The Link feature is used to add information from a file created in another program to a Word file.

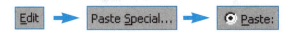

Notes:

- The embedded information becomes part of the Word (destination) file, but the source program can be launched from the embedded information.

1 In the source file, copy the desired information to the clipboard.

2 In the Word destination file, click **Edit**, **Paste Special**. The Paste Special dialog box opens.

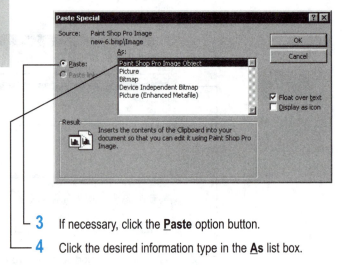

3 If necessary, click the **Paste** option button.

4 Click the desired information type in the **As** list box.

58

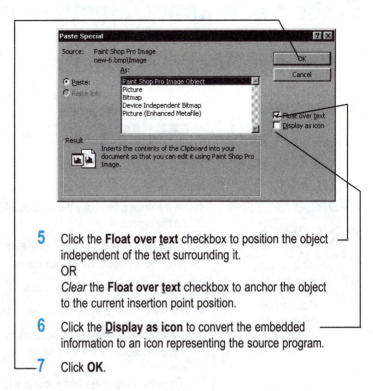

5 Click the **Float over text** checkbox to position the object independent of the text surrounding it.
OR
Clear the **Float over text** checkbox to anchor the object to the current insertion point position.

6 Click the **Display as icon** to convert the embedded information to an icon representing the source program.

7 Click **OK**.

Edit an Embedded Object

Double-click the object to launch the source program.

Notes:

- The linked information remains part of the source file, so when the source file is changed, the information in the Word file (the destination file) is automatically updated.

1 In the source file, copy the desired information to the clipboard.

2 In the Word destination file, click **Edit**, **Paste Special**. The Paste Special dialog box opens.

3 Click the **Paste link** option button.

4 Click the desired information type in the **As** list box.

5 Click the **Float over text** checkbox to position the object independent of the text surrounding it.
OR
Clear the **Float over text** checkbox to anchor the object to the current insertion point position.

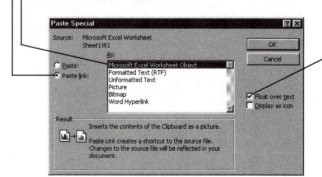

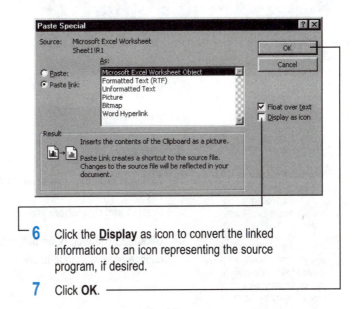

6 Click the **Display** as icon to convert the linked information to an icon representing the source program, if desired.

7 Click **OK**.

Edit a Linked Object

Double-click the object to open the source file.

Styles: Apply a Style

Styles are used to save or apply a set of character and paragraph formats to selected text.

Notes:

- Word comes with a number of pre-formatted styles. You may create and save your own.

- If you use styles in a document and later decide to modify them, the text that was formatted with the style will also change.

Toolbar

1   Click and drag over text to select it.
    OR
    Point to and click where you intend to type new text.

2   Click the Style drop-down button  and choose desired style to apply.

Dialog Box

Format ➡ Style...

1   Click and drag over text to select it.
    OR
    Point and click where you intend to type new text.

2 Click **Format**, **Style** to open the Styles dialog box.

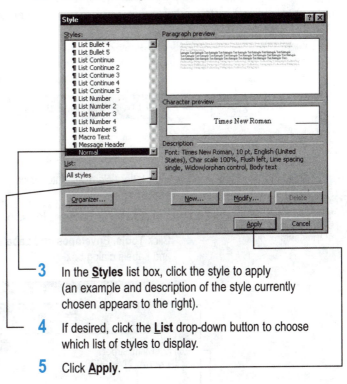

3 In the **Styles** list box, click the style to apply (an example and description of the style currently chosen appears to the right).

4 If desired, click the **List** drop-down button to choose which list of styles to display.

5 Click **Apply**.

Envelopes

Use the envelope feature to quickly format, address, and print an envelope.

Notes:

- You can change the return address in the User Information tab of the Options dialog box.

1 View letter (Word will automatically find the addressee)
OR
Select name and address to use on envelope, if desired.

2 Click **Tools**, **Envelopes and Labels** to open the Envelopes and Labels dialog box.

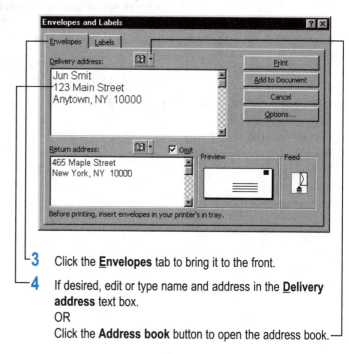

3 Click the **Envelopes** tab to bring it to the front.

4 If desired, edit or type name and address in the **Delivery address** text box.
OR
Click the **Address book** button to open the address book.

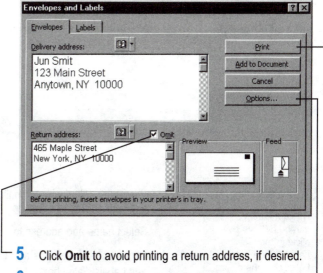

5 Click **Omit** to avoid printing a return address, if desired.

6 If desired, click **Options** to change envelope size, font type and size, or position of address.

7 Click **Print** to send the envelope to the printer
OR
Click **Add to Document** to add a page containing the envelope to the current document.

65

Labels

Use the labels feature to create and format a sheet of repeating labels or a single label.

Tools ➔ Envelopes and Labels...

1 View letter (Word will automatically find the addressee)
OR
Select name and address to use on labels, if desired.

2 Click **Tools**, **Envelopes and Labels** to open the Envelopes and Labels dialog box.

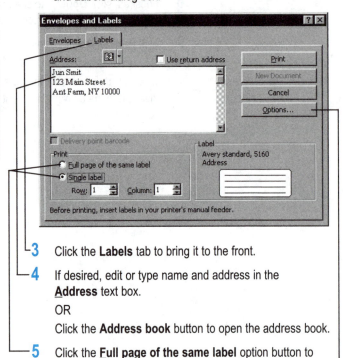

3 Click the **Labels** tab to bring it to the front.

4 If desired, edit or type name and address in the **Address** text box.
OR
Click the **Address book** button to open the address book.

5 Click the **Full page of the same label** option button to repeat the address information
OR
Click the **Single label** option button and specify where you want to place the label in the Row and Column text boxes.

6 To change the label size, click the **Options** button to open the Label Options dialog box.

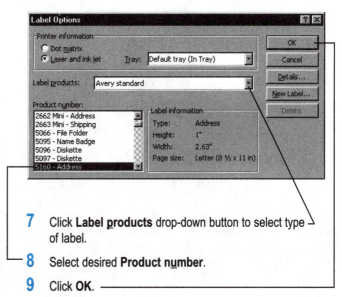

7 Click **Label products** drop-down button to select type of label.

8 Select desired **Product number**.

9 Click **OK**.

10 Click **Print** to send the labels to the printer.
OR
Click **New Document** to create new labels.

Excel

Microsoft Office's spreadsheet application. It can be used to track and analyze numerical data for display on screen or in printed format. Excel is designed to help you record and calculate data, and present it in a clear and attractive manner. Excel provides you with various chart and layout options to enhance your spreadsheets. This book will help you to take full advantage of Excel's many abilities.

About the Excel Window

Excel provides an interface (graphical tools and controls) for working with worksheet data. This topic will help you to identify the purpose of the tools and indicators that appear in the Excel window.

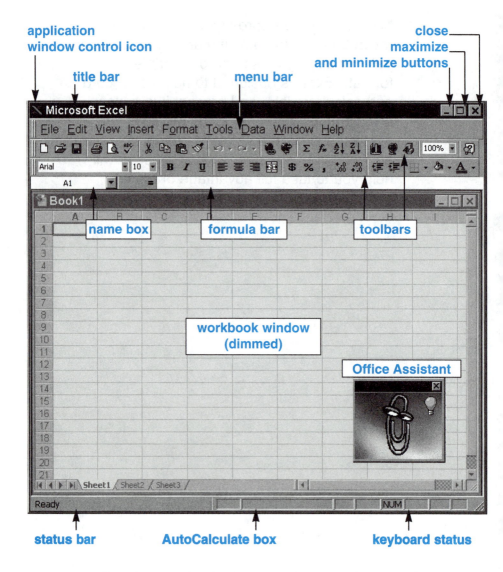

The Excel 97 Application as It Appears When You Open It

- In the illustration, there are two sets of **close**, **maximize** and **minimize** buttons: One for the Excel application window, and one for the workbook window. The **maximize** button will appear as a **restore** button if the window has already been maximized.

- If the workbook was maximized in the illustration, its name (Book1) would appear in the Excel application title bar, and the workbook title bar would not be available. *(See Window Controls for information about maximizing and restoring windows.)*

The Microsoft Excel Window

Microsoft Excel title bar: Displays the program name (Microsoft Excel), and may also display the file name of an open workbook window, if the workbook is maximized. You can drag the title bar to move the window, or double-click it to maximize the window.

Application window control icon: Click it to access a drop-down menu of commands that control the position and size of the application window.

Close, maximize, and minimize buttons: Click buttons to close, maximize, or minimize the Excel window.

Menu bar: Displays menu names which, when clicked, display drop-down menus.

Toolbars: Click buttons on toolbar to select commands quickly, without opening a menu or dialog box.

Name box: Displays the cell reference of the active cell.

Formula bar: Provides a space for typing or editing cell data.

Status bar: Displays information about the current mode, selected command, or option. The right side of the status bar shows the **keyboard status**. For example, NUM indicates the numeric keyboard is active (number lock). The middle of the status bar contains the **AutoCalculate box**, which displays the result of a selected AutoCalculate function (such as SUM or AVERAGE) when applied to a selected range of cells.

Office Assistant: Appears when you open Excel, and can answer your questions about how to perform a task.

Workbook window: Appears in, and is restricted to, the Excel window. Workbook windows contain the data that you enter in worksheets (purposely muted in this illustration). You can open multiple workbook windows within Excel.

About Cells

Cells are areas in a worksheet in which you store data. You refer to cell locations by specifying their column and row positions in the worksheet. This is called a cell reference. You can enter text, values, and formulas in cells.

Notes:

- Each cell is defined by the intersection of a row and a column (e.g., A3, denoting column A, row 3). The cell's location is called a **cell reference** (or cell address).

- When you open a new workbook, it usually contains multiple worksheets. Each worksheet contains 256 columns and 65,536 rows. Therefore, each worksheet contains 17,033,216 cells!

- **Columns** are labeled A through IV, while **rows** are numbered 1 - 65,536.

- Each cell can store up to 32,000 characters.

- To select a cell, just click it, or press any arrow key in the direction of the cell you want to select. For more information about moving around in a worksheet, see *Navigate Worksheet*.

About Cell Locations

In the illustration below, cell B2 is the selected cell in Sheet1. You know this because:

- The reference B2 appears in the **name box**.
- Excel has outlined the column heading B and the row heading 2.
- Sheet1 is the highlighted tab in the workbook window.
  The contents of the selected cell appear in the formula bar.

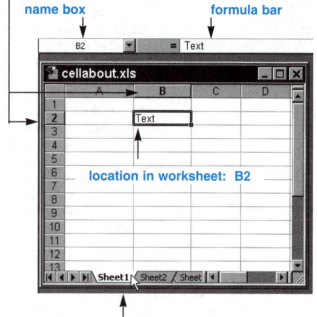

Cell Location in a Workbook

Notes:

- A **control** is any graphical element that allows you to perform an action or specify a setting. Excel changes the shape of the mouse pointer when you rest it on a cell control, such as a cell border or fill handle.

- A **cell reference** indicates a cell's location. Cell references are often used in formulas to calculate values stored in other cells. *(See About Formulas and About References.)*

About Cell Properties and Controls

Cells are defined by the intersection of a column and a row. Therefore, the dimensions of a cell are defined by the column width and the row height. All cells have borders and fill properties. Selected cells have darkened borders and a fill handle (controls). These controls let you perform actions on the cell with the mouse.

Border control: You can drag the border of the selected cell to move its contents.

Border style: You can apply line styles to one or more of the borders of a cell.

Fill: You can color or shade a cell to distinguish it from other cells.

Fill handle: You can drag the fill handle of selected cells to extend their content as a series, or, for a single cell, to copy its content to adjacent cells.

Height/width: You can change the column width and row height to adjust the size of a cell.

Location: You can identify the location of the selected cell by reading its cell reference in the **name box** (see illustration on previous page). You can insert cell references in formulas. For example, the formula =B2+C4 adds the values stored in those cells.

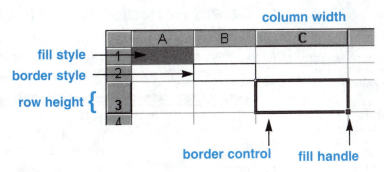

Cell Properties and Controls

Select Cells, Columns, and Rows

When working with worksheets, you will need to select a cell or range of cells to complete a variety of tasks. A range may consist of adjacent or nonadjacent cells. You can also name and select named cell ranges. Keyboard shortcuts for selecting cells can be found in online Help, on the Index tab, under "keyboard shortcuts."

Notes:

- Excel will scroll the worksheet when you drag the selection beyond the visible area of the worksheet. The first cell you select becomes the active cell (cell A2 in the illustration).

Select Adjacent Cell Range

1 Click first cell you want to select.

2 Drag mouse in direction of cells to include in selection.

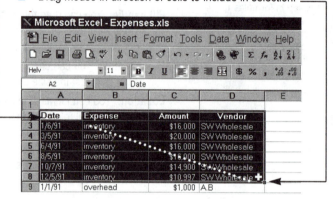

Notes:

- The first cell in the last range you select becomes the active cell (cell C2 in the illustration).

- Selecting nonadjacent cell ranges or multiple selections is often used to designate data to be included in a chart.

Select Nonadjacent Cell Range

1 Click first cell and drag in direction of cells to select.

2 Press and hold **Ctrl** while dragging through additional ranges to include in your selection.

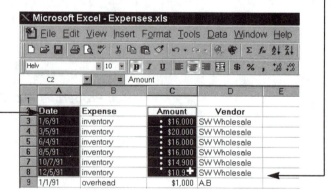

Select Entire Column or Row

- Click row or column heading to select.

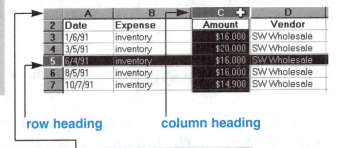

row heading   **column heading**

Notes:

Name a Range

- You can also name nonadjacent ranges, as shown on the previous page.

1 Select the range to name.

2 Click in the **name box** and type descriptive name.

NOTE: Range names cannot include spaces. They may contain uppercase and lowercase letters, numbers, and most punctuation characters. The underscore character is useful for simulating a space, as in "inventory_expenses."

- You might want to name ranges that you frequently chart or print.

- You can also use the **Go To** command (**F5**) to select named ranges.

3 Press **Enter**.

Select a Named Range

- Click in **name box**, then click name to select.

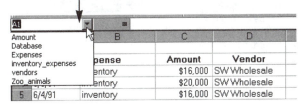

75

Adjust and Hide Columns

Data appears in cells defined in part by the column width. You can control the width of columns as well as hide them using the procedures in this topic. You can also adjust columns while previewing how your workbook will print *(see Print Preview)*.

Format ➡ Column

Notes:

- In **step 2**, the pointer indicates when you can perform the action. It must be a cross with left- and right-facing arrows, as shown in the illustration to the right.

- The width of the column is measured in the number of characters of the standard font.

Change Column Width Using the Mouse

1 **To set width of multiple columns in one step:**

Drag through column headings of columns to change.

OR

Press **Ctrl** and click column headings to change.

2 Rest pointer on right border of any selected column heading.

Pointer becomes a cross with left- and right-facing arrows.

3 Drag pointer left or right to decrease or increase the column size.

Excel displays width (in characters) in a pop-up box.

	C2	▼	=	33333 Width: 8.57

	A	B	C ✛ D
1			
2			########
3			

column headings   **cell pointer**

Notes:

- In **step 1**, you can select multiple columns, but each column will adjust to the same size.

- In **step 2**, the pointer indicates when you can perform the action. It must be a cross with left- and right-facing arrows.

Automatically Size Column to Fit Largest Entry

1 Rest pointer on right border of column heading.

Pointer becomes a cross with arrows facing left and right.

2 Double-click.

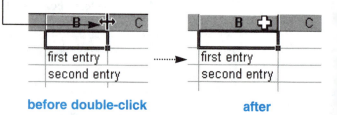

B ▶✛ C	B ✛ C
first entry	first entry
second entry	second entry

before double-click   **after**

76

Hide Columns by Dragging

1 Rest pointer on right border of any selected column heading.

Pointer becomes a cross with left- and right-facing arrows.

2 Drag pointer left beyond its own left border.

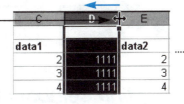

before   **after**

Display Hidden Columns by Dragging

1 Rest pointer just to the right of column heading border.

Pointer becomes a cross with a double vertical line and left and right-facing arrows.

2 Drag pointer right to display the hidden column.

before   **after**

Adjust Columns Using the Menu

1 Select column(s) to adjust.
2 Click **Format** menu, then point to or click **Column**.
3 Click desired column command.

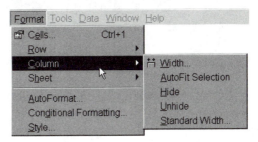

Align Data in Cells

Aligns cell data horizontally and vertically; applies text controls (wrap text in cells, shrink text to fit, merge cells); orients text in a variety of angles.

Format → Cells... — Alignment

Notes:

- If no alignment is set, Excel applies the **General alignment** which automatically left-aligns text and right-aligns values.

- If text cannot fit in a cell, you can increase the column width or select the **Shrink to fit** option *(see next page)*.

Align Cell Data Using Toolbar

1 Select cell(s) to align.

> *NOTE: To select cells that are nonadjacent, you can press **Ctrl** and click or drag through cells to include in the selection.*

2 Click desired alignment button on the Formatting toolbar:

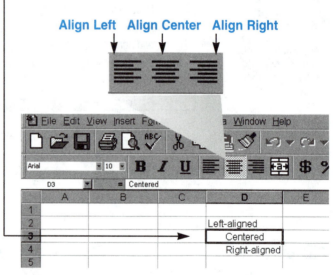

Horizontal Alignment Examples

Notes:

Notes:

- A merged cell is one or more consecutive cells combined into one cell address.

- When you merge cells, only the contents of the upper-left cell are retained, and that cell becomes the cell reference.

Merge and Center

1 Select cell containing data and extend selection to include cells in which data will be centered.

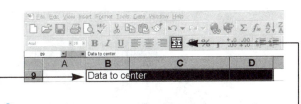

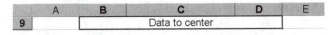

2 Click **Merge and Center** button on toolbar.

Merge and Center Example

Notes:

- Alignment options:

Horizontal and **Vertical** — sets alignment of text in cells.

Wrap text — inserts line breaks when needed and increases the row height automatically.

Shrink to fit — sets the characters to fit the column width automatically.

Merge cells — joins selected cells. The contents of the upper-left cell are retained, and that cell becomes the cell reference.

Indent — offsets data away from the left side of cell. Increments are in width of characters.

Orientation — sets the rotation of text. Increments are measured in degrees.

Menu Alignment Options

You can set alignment options from a dialog box.

1 Select cells.
2 Click **Format** menu, then click **Cells**.
3 Click the **Alignment** tab.
4 Select desired options and click **OK**.

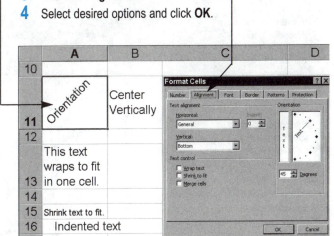

Menu Alignment Examples

Clear Cell Contents

Clears cell contents without adjusting surrounding cells. Using menu commands, you can clear cell formats, contents, comments, or all of these items.

Notes:

- In **step 1**, Excel will perform the clear command on all the cells you select in one step.

- In **step 2**, **right-click** means to press the right mouse button when the pointer is resting on any cell you have selected in step 1.

- After you clear cells, you can the click **Edit** menu, then **Undo** to reverse the operation.

- In the illustration on this page, notice that after the **Clear Contents** command, the surrounding cells do not change position, and the format of the cell is retained (bold font in example).

Clear Cell Contents

Removes the contents (data and formulas) and leaves the cells blank in the worksheet, without removing formats or comments that may be applied to the cells.

1 Select cells to clear.

> NOTE: To select cells that are nonadjacent, you can press **Ctrl** and click or drag through cells to include in the selection.

2 Press **Delete**.

OR

- Right-click any selected cell.

  A shortcut menu appears.

- Click **Clear Contents**.

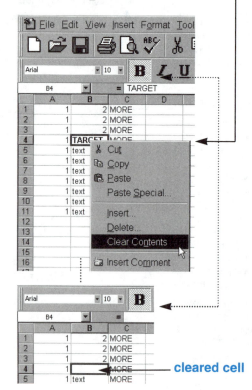

cleared cell

Clear Cell Options Using Menu

Clears cell formats, contents, comments, or all of these items.

1 Select cells to clear.

> *NOTE:* *To select cells that are nonadjacent, you can press **Ctrl** and click or drag through cells to include in the selection.*

2 Click **E_dit_** menu, then **Cle_ar_**.

3 Click one of the following:

All	to clear formats, contents, and comments.
F_ormats_	to clear only formats, such as border styles and font attributes.
Contents	to clear just the contents of the cell.
Co_mments_	to clear just the comment attached to the cell.

Excel clears the cells as directed by your command.

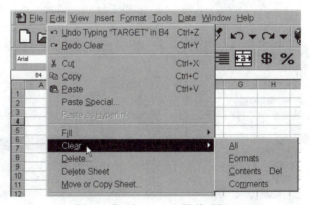

Clear Options on Edit Menu

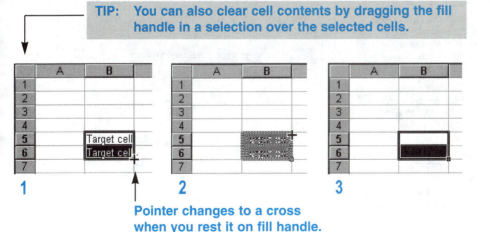

TIP: You can also clear cell contents by dragging the fill handle in a selection over the selected cells.

1 **2** **3**

Pointer changes to a cross when you rest it on fill handle.

Copy Cell Contents

You can copy the data in one cell to other cells in a variety of ways. The method you choose often depends upon the location of the data and the destination.

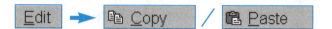

Notes:

- Using menu commands to copy cells is best when both the source and destination cells are *not* in the same viewing area.

- In **step 2**, the flashing dashed outline remains until you press **Esc**. This indicates you can repeat the paste operation.

- In **step 2** and **step 4**, you can also right-click the selection to select the **Copy** and **Paste** commands from a shortcut menu.

- **Caution:** When you paste data, existing data in the destination cells will be replaced. You can click **Edit** menu, then **Undo** to reverse the paste operation, however.

- In **step 4**, to avoid overwriting data, click **Insert** menu, then click **Copied Cells**. The Insert Paste dialog box will appear from which you can choose the direction to shift the existing cells.

Copy Cell Data Using Menu Commands

1 Select cells to copy.

2 Click **Edit** menu, then click **Copy**.
A flashing dashed outline appears around data.

3 Select destination cell.

4 Click **Edit** menu, then click **Paste**.

5 Repeat steps 3 and 4 to repeat paste operation.

6 Press **Esc** to turn off the paste option.

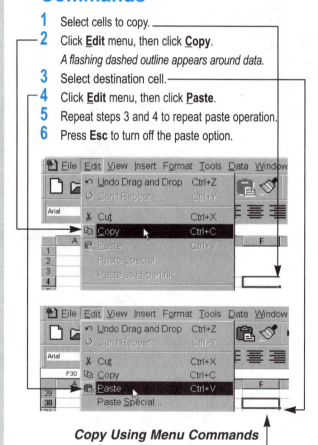

Copy Using Menu Commands

Tip: If you intend to paste the data once, you can bypass steps 4-6 and just press Enter.

Copy Cell Contents by Dragging Cell Border

1 Select cell(s) to copy.

2 Point to any border of selected cell(s).

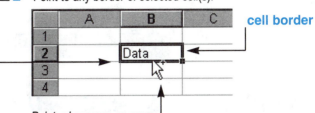

cell border

Pointer becomes an arrow.

3 Press **Ctrl** and drag border outline to new location.

4 Release mouse button.

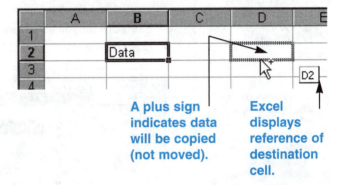

A plus sign indicates data will be copied (not moved).

Excel displays reference of destination cell.

Copy Cell Contents by Dragging Fill Handle

Crosshair appears when pointer rests on fill handle.

1 Select cell(s) to copy, then point to fill handle.

A crosshair appears.

2 Drag crosshair to extend border over adjacent cells to fill.

3 Release mouse button.

Excel copies data into all cells within extended border.

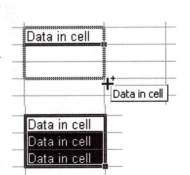

Delete Cells, Columns, or Rows

You can delete cells, entire columns, or rows from a worksheet. Existing cells adjust to take the place of the removed cells. Do not confuse Delete with Clear. Clearing cells removes only the data, while deleting cells removes the cells from the worksheet.

Notes:

- In **step 1**, to select cells that are nonadjacent, you can press **Ctrl** and click or drag through cells to include in the selection.

- If deleted cells have been used in formulas, the formulas will display #REF! error messages. If references to adjusted cells exist in formulas, Excel adjusts the formulas, even if the reference types are absolute.

- **Caution:** You can lose data with the delete action. However, you can click **Edit** menu, then **Undo** to reverse the action.

Delete Cells Using Menu

1 Select cells to delete.

2 Click **Edit** menu, then click **Delete**.
   The Delete dialog box appears.

3 Select direction you want existing cells to shift.

4 Click **OK**.

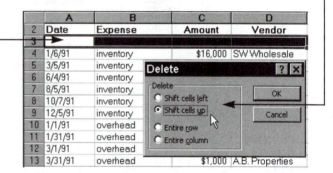

TIP: In step 2, you can also right-click any selected cell, then click **Delete** from the shortcut menu that appears.

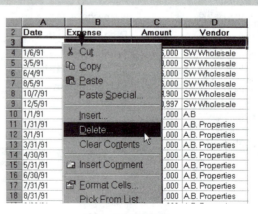

Shortcut Menu

84

Delete Entire Column or Row

1 Click row or column heading to select.

2 Click **Edit** menu, then click **Delete**.

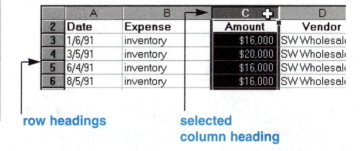

row headings

selected column heading

TIP: You can also delete cells by pressing Shift and dragging the fill handle in a selection over the selected cells.

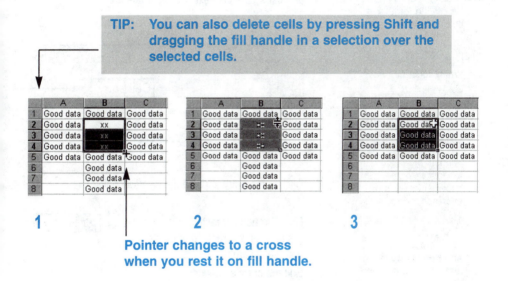

1 **2** **3**

Pointer changes to a cross when you rest it on fill handle.

85

Edit Cell Data

What you have typed in a cell can be changed (edited) with a variety of techniques. When cell editing is enabled, the formula bar displays extra controls (buttons) and displays the cell contents both in the cell and in the formula bar.

Notes:

* There are three ways you can begin to edit a cell entry:

  Double-click the cell.

  Click the cell, then click in the formula bar.

  Click the cell, then press **F2**.

* When editing:

  Excel displays a flashing cursor that indicates where new input will be inserted.

  You can press the **Ins** key to toggle between insert and overwrite mode.

  The formula bar changes to include the **Cancel**, **Enter** and **Edit Formula** buttons illustrated on the next page.

  You can insert data from the Clipboard, by pressing **Ctrl+V.**

Edit a Cell Entry by Double-Clicking

1 Double-click cell containing data to edit.

Excel displays a flashing insertion pointer in the entry and extra controls next to the formula bar.

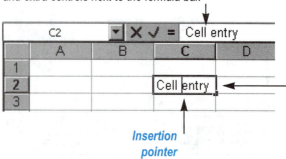

Insertion
pointer

2 Click in the entry to place the insertion pointer.

OR

Drag through characters to select (next action will replace or delete your selection).

3 Edit the entry as needed:

* Type characters to insert.

* Press **Del** to delete characters to the right of insertion pointer or to delete the selection.

* Press **Backspace** to delete character to the left of the insertion pointer or to delete the selection.

4 Press **Enter**.

OR

Click ✔ on formula bar.

Replace a Cell Entry

1 Select cell containing data to replace.
2 Type new data.
3 Press **Enter**.
   OR
   Click ✓ on formula bar.

Cancel Changes to a Cell Entry

Prior to entering the change:

- Press **Esc**.
  OR
  Click ✗ on formula bar.

Formula Bar and Related Controls

Name box . . . . Displays cell reference (C2) of the data you are editing.

Cancel button ✗ . . . . Lets you cancel a revision before completing it.

Enter button ✓ . . . . Lets you complete the revision with a mouse click.

Edit Formula button . . . . . Provides help when editing formulas.

Formula bar . . . . Lets you edit the cell content.

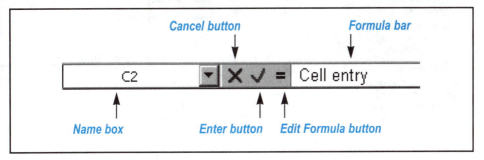

Formula Bar and Related Controls

Enter Cell Data

Entering data is very straightforward. There are, however, many techniques for entering data of different types, such as dates, times, fractions, percents, and formulas.

Enter Text or Whole Numbers

1 Select cell to receive entry.

2 Type the text or whole number.

A flashing insertion pointer appears after the data you type, and the formula bar also displays your entry.

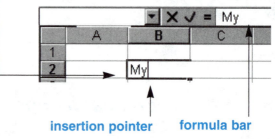

insertion pointer   **formula bar**

3 Press **Enter**.

OR

Click ✓ on formula bar.

Excel completes the entry and selects the cell below it.

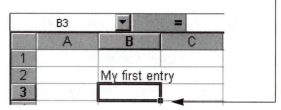

To cancel the entry before completing it:

- Press **Esc**.

OR

Click ✗ on formula bar.

> **Tip:** To enter identical data in multiple cells, select cells, type data, then press **Ctrl+Enter**.

- Excel will automatically apply special number formats to what you have typed, when you type the value in a special format. For example, if you type a zero, a space, and a fraction, Excel will automatically apply the fraction format and display the value as 1/2.

- Dates and times may be displayed as a combination of text and numbers. However, Excel stores dates and times as serial values and calculates these values accordingly. For example, Excel stores Jan-1-1997 as 35431, and the date Jan-1,1900 as 1.

Enter Special Kinds of Data

1 Select cell to receive entry.

2 Type the data as shown in samples in the table below.

A flashing insertion pointer appears after the data you type, and the formula bar also displays your entry.

3 Press **Enter**.

Category:	Example of what to type:
Currency	$25,000.25
Date	6/24/97
	24-Jun
	24-Jun-97
	Jun-97
Date and time	6/24/97 10 AM
Fraction	0 1/2
Label	text
Mixed number	1 1/2
Number	25
Number as label	="25"
Percent	25%
Time	10 AM
Formula (simple)	=A1+B1

Tip: To enter today's date, press Ctrl+; (semicolon).

- AutoComplete will not assist in entering numbers.

- Another way to use AutoComplete is to right-click the cell to receive the data, click **Pick from List**, then click the data you want to enter. This method lets you input data entirely with the mouse.

How AutoComplete Works

The AutoComplete feature assists you when you enter repeating text in a column.

1 Select cell to receive text.

2 Type part of the text.

Excel automatically completes the entry (see highlighted text in illustration below) based on data that it finds in the column.

Categories
vegetable
stone
vegetable

NOTE: Type over the highlighted text, if you want to change it.

3 Press **Enter**.

Format Numbers

When you enter a value, Excel applies the format it thinks appropriate to your entry *(see Enter Cell Data)*. You can apply common number formats from the Formatting toolbar, such as Currency and Percentage; or you can select specific number formats using menu commands and the Format Cells dialog box.

Format ➡ 🖅 Cells... ⌐ Number ⌐

Notes:

• When you change a number format, Excel does not change the underlying value.

• If the number cannot fit in the cell after you change the number format, Excel displays ####### (pound signs) in the cell. To fix this problem, increase the column width *(see Adjust and Hide Columns)*, or select the **Shrink to fit** option*(see Align Data in Cells)*.

• You can format a number when you enter it, by typing specific symbols, such as a $ or %.

Format Numbers Using Toolbar

1 Select cell(s) containing values to format.

> *NOTE:* *To select cells that are nonadjacent, you can press **Ctrl** and click or drag through cells to include in the selection.*

2 Click desired number format button on the Formatting toolbar:

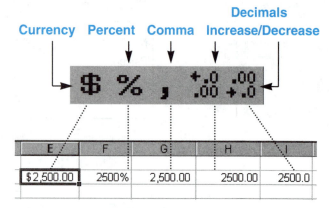

Sample Results Using Buttons on the Formatting Toolbar

- By default, Excel applies the General number format, unless you enter the number with special characters *(see Enter Cell Data)*.

- In **step 4**, the selected category indicates the current number format of the selected cell. If more than one cell is selected, and they have different number formats, no category will be selected automatically.

- The **Custom** category contains templates for all the number formats. You can select a format that is closest to the desired format, then modify it as desired. In the sample below, the custom format (date and time) shows the full year 1900.

- You can hide data in a cell by creating, then applying a custom number format. To create the format: From the **Format Cells** dialog box, select **Custom** in **Category** box, then type three semicolons (;;;) in the **Type** box.

- Excel displays help for the selected category near the bottom of the dialog box.

Format Numbers Using Menu Commands

1 Select cell(s) containing values to format.

> *NOTE:* *To select cells that are nonadjacent, you can press **Ctrl** and click or drag through cells to include in the selection.*

2 Click **Format** menu, then click **Cells**.

3 Click the **Number** tab.

4 Select category of number format in **Category** list.

Excel displays options for the selected category.

5 Select options for the category you have selected.

Excel displays sample in Sample box.

6 Click **OK** when done.

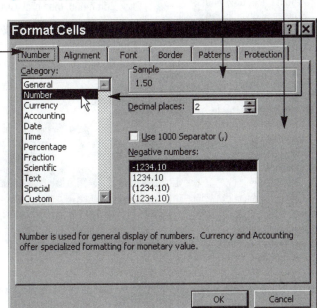

Category	Value	Comment
General	1.5	
Number	1.50	
Currency	$1.50	
Accounting	$ 1.50	
Date	January 1, 1900	*first day of century*
Time	1/1/00 12:00 PM	*first day and a half of century*
Percentage	150.00%	*you can set decimal places*
Fraction	1 1/2	
Scientific	1.50E+00	
Text	1.5	
Special	00002	*zip code*
	(718) 980-0999	*phone number*
	000-00-0002	*social security number*
Custom	1/1/1900 12:00 PM	*customized date and time*

Sample Number Formats

Move Cell Contents

You can move the data in one cell to other cells in a variety of ways. The best method to choose depends upon the location of the source data and its destination.

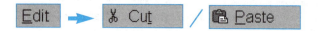

Move Cell Contents Using Menu Commands

1 Select cells to move.

2 Click **Edit** menu, then click **Cut**.
   A flashing dashed outline appears around selected cell.

3 Select destination cell.

4 Click **Edit** menu, then click **Paste**.
   OR
   Press **Enter**.

Move Using Menu Commands

Notes:

- The drag border method is best when the source and destination cells are nearby.

- In **step 3**, "drag" means to press and hold the left mouse button while moving the mouse.

- In **step 3**, to avoid overwriting data in destination cells, press **Ctrl+Shift** while dragging cell border. Existing cells will shift to accommodate new data.

Move Cell Contents by Dragging Cell Border

1 Select cell(s) containing data to move.

2 Point to any border of selected cell(s).

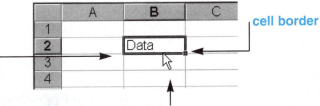

cell border

Pointer becomes a solid arrow.

3 Drag border outline to new location.

4 Release mouse button.

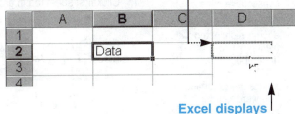

Excel displays reference of destination cell.

Notes:

- You can also use menu commands (**Edit**, **Cut** and **Edit**, **Paste**) to move a cell's content.

- If you make a mistake, you can click the **Edit** menu, then click **Undo**. Excel lets you undo multiple actions, not just your last.

Move Part of a Cell's Contents into Another Cell

1 Double-click cell containing data to move.

A flashing insertion pointer appears.

2 Drag through data to select it. ⟶

3 Press **Ctrl+X** (Cut).

4 Double-click destination cell and click where data will be inserted.

OR

Select cell to be overwritten by data.

5 Press **Ctrl+V** (Paste).

Excel highlights data in cell.

Sheet Tabs

Sheet tabs let you organize and work with multiple worksheets within a single workbook file. You can select, group, insert, rename, delete, move, and copy sheet tabs.

Notes:

- In **step 2**, you can also press **Shift** and click to select consecutive sheets.

  Grouped sheets appear highlighted (white), while ungrouped sheets appear grey. When sheets are grouped, The word "[Group]" appears after the workbook name on the title bar.

- You can also ungroup sheets by clicking any sheet tab that is not currently grouped.

Group and Ungroup Sheet Tabs

When you group sheets, data and formatting changes made to the active sheet are repeated in the grouped sheets.

1 Click first sheet tab in group.

2 Press **Ctrl** and click each sheet tab to add to group.

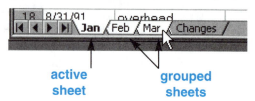

active sheet　　**grouped sheets**

3 Click any grouped sheet tab to make it active.

To ungroup sheet tabs:

- Right-click any grouped sheet, then click **Ungroup Sheets** on the shortcut menu that appears.

Notes:

- **Caution:** Be careful when deleting worksheets, because you cannot undo this action.

Delete Sheet Tabs

1 Right-click sheet tab to delete, then click **Delete** on the shortcut menu that appears.

2 Click **OK** to confirm the action.

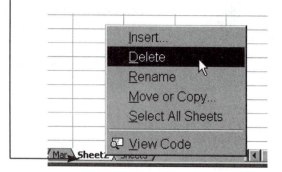

Notes:

- In **step 1**, you can insert multiple worksheets by first selecting (grouping) the number of sheets you want to insert, then right-clicking on that group.

- In **step 2**, you can also insert special items, such as chart and macro sheets.

- From the **Spreadsheet Solutions** tab, you can select a custom template.

Insert a New Sheet

1 Right-click any sheet tab, then click **Insert** on the shortcut menu that appears.

The Insert dialog box appears.

2 Click **Worksheet** icon, then click **OK**.

3 Rename and move sheet tab as desired.

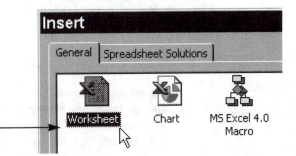

Notes:

- In **step 1**, you can also right-click the tab to rename, then click **Rename** from the shortcut menu that appears.

- Worksheet names may contain spaces and punctuation.

Rename a Sheet

1 Double-click sheet tab to rename.

Excel highlights the sheet tab name.

2 Type new name, then click anywhere in worksheet.

Notes:

- When you copy a sheet, Excel renames the new sheet by adding a number to it. For example, a copy of **Sheet1** may be named **Sheet1 (2)**. You can, of course, rename the sheet.

Move and Copy Sheets

1 Select sheet(s) to move or copy.

Excel highlights the the sheet tab names.

2 To move sheets, drag selection to desired location.

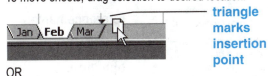

triangle marks insertion point

OR

To copy sheets, press **Ctrl** and drag selection to desired location.

plus sign indicates copy

About Formulas

You can enter and build formulas to calculate values stored in your worksheet. Here, you will receive basic information about formulas — formula location, formula parts, controlling the order of operation, and formula examples.

Notes:

- A **formula** is an instruction to calculate numbers.

- You can set Excel to display formulas in cells: Click **Tools** menu, then **Options**; click the **View** tab, and select the **Formulas** Window option.

Formula Location

You will enter a formula in the cell where the result should appear. As you type the formula, it appears in the cell and in the formula bar. After you enter a formula, the result is displayed in the cell, and the formula is displayed in the formula bar.

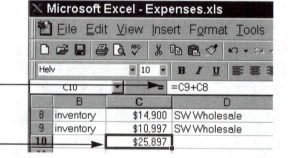

formula

formula result

Notes:

- **References** and **reference names** indicate the location of cells in a worksheet.

- **Functions** are predefined formulas that use arguments in fixed locations to perform calculations.

- **Operators** tell Excel the kind of calculation to perform.

- **Parentheses** affect the order of operations and must be used in pairs.

Formula Parts

Formulas always begin with an equal sign (**=**) and often contain the elements shown in bold type in the following sample formulas:

numbers	=A1+**25**
cell references	=**A1**-25
reference names	=A1***Salary**
functions	=**Sum(A1:A10)**+Salary
operators	=A1**/**2**+**25*****22**-**3
parentheses	=**(**24+A1**)**/2**%**

Control the Order of Operations in Formulas

It is important to consider the order of mathematical operations when preparing formulas. Excel will perform the operation in your formulas in the following order:

- operations enclosed in parentheses ( )
- percentage %
- exponential ^
- multiplication and division * /
- addition and subtraction + -
- concatenation (connection of text strings) &
- comparisons = < > <= >= <>

Notes:

- Some of the examples contain named references. You must first name a range, before you can refer to its name in a formula. However, Excel will let you use names automatically when labels exist next to numbers in your worksheet.

Formula Examples

This is a list of common formulas followed by a brief explanation:

=A1+25 — adds the contents of cell A1 to the constant 25.

=A1-25 — from the content of cell A1, subtracts 25.

=A1*TotalSalary — multiplies the content of cell A1 by the content of the cell named TotalSalary.

=Sum(A1:A10)+TotalSalary — adds the content of the cell named TotalSalary to the sum of the range of cells A1 through A10.

=A10+(25*TotalSalary) — multiplies the content of the cell named TotalSalary by 25, then adds that to the content of cell A10.

=A10^3 — multiplies the content of A10 by itself 3 times (exponentially).

=2%*A10 — two percent of the content of cell A10.

=(Min(Salary)+Max(Salary))/2 — adds the minimum value in the range of cells named Salary to the maximum value in that range, and divides it by 2.

=A10 & " " & A11 — combines the text in cells A10 and A11 with a space between them. If A10 contains HELLO and A11 contains THERE, the result would be HELLO THERE.

=IF(A1<>0,A1*B10," ") — If value in cell A1 is not zero, multiplies A1 by value in B10, otherwise displays blank text.

Create Formulas (Simple)

You will enter and build formulas to calculate values stored in your worksheet. Here, you will receive basic information about building formulas, pasting names into a formula, and inserting references in formulas.

Notes:

- In **step 1**, select a cell in which you want the result of the calculation to appear.

- In **step 2**, when you type the equal sign, controls appear on the formula bar. These controls are described on the next page.

- In the illustration, the simple formula =25*A1 multiplies the value in A1 by 25.

- You can repeat the process of inserting a reference and typing an operator until all the cells you want to calculate are included in the formula. For information about changing a formula, see *Edit Formulas*.

- If you decide you want to start over and cancel the entry, press **Esc**.

Build Formula (Add References)

1 Select cells to receive formula.

2 Type an equal sign (=).
The equal sign appears in the cell and in the formula bar.

3 Type the formula *(for examples see About Formulas)*.

To insert a reference in formula by pointing:

- Click cell containing value to reference.
  A dashed line appears around the cell, and Excel inserts the reference in your formula.

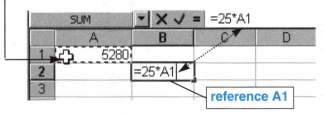

reference A1

4 Type next part of formula. If formula is complete, go to step 5, below.
Excel removes dashed outline, and what you type appears in cell and formula bar.

5 Press **Enter**.
OR
Click ✓ on formula bar.
Excel calculates the formula and displays the result in the cell.

Paste a Named Range into a Formula

1 Place insertion point in formula.
2 Click **Insert** menu, then click or point to **Name**.
3 Click **Paste** on the submenu that appears.
4 Click name to paste in formula, then click **OK**.

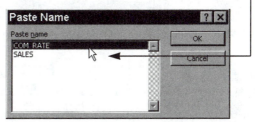

Create Formula, Insert Cell References, and Change Reference Type

1 If you wish, first type the data in a new worksheet as shown in the illustration below. Then create the typical formula in C7 that calculates the commission (=B2*C5).

	A	B	C	D
1		SALES COMMISSION		
2	COM RATE	4.00%		
3				
4		ELMHURST	CADDY	WUILLS
5	SALES	640000	340000	540000
6	BONUS	2000	1000	2000
7	COMMISSION	25600		
8	TOTAL COMP	27600		

2 Select cell to receive formula (C7).
3 Type **=** to start the formula.
4 Click cell to insert as reference in formula (B2).

To change the inserted reference to absolute:

- Press **F4**.

  Reference changes to absolute (B2 becomes B2).

5 Type desired operator (*****) .
6 Click next cell to insert as reference in formula (C5).
7 Press **Enter** to complete the formula.

Create Functions

Functions are predefined formulas that perform specific kinds of calculations, such as finding an average or future value. Functions require arguments — the data needed to perform the calculation. To make it easy to create a function, Excel provides the Paste Function Wizard.

Paste Function button

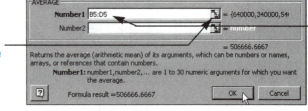

Functions list on formula bar

Insert a Function Using Function Wizard

1 Select cell in which function will be created.

2 Click **Paste Function** button on Standard toolbar.

The Paste Function dialog box appears.

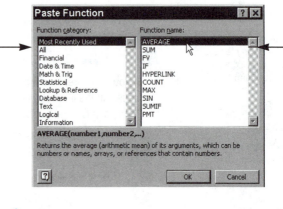

3 Select desired category in **Function category** list.

4 Select desired function in **Function name** list, then click **OK**.

A dialog box specific to the function you selected appears.

Dialog Collapse button

5 Insert cell references or values in **Number** boxes that appear.

> NOTE: You can click the **Collapse Dialog** button on the right side of the **Number** box, then select the cells to calculate directly from the worksheet. (See Use Dialog Box Controls.)

6 Click **OK** when done.

Notes:

- In **step 1**, if you double-click the cell, then click the **Paste Function** button, you will insert a new function into your existing function at the insertion point.

- In **step 3**, refer to illustration on bottom of previous page.

Edit a Function

1 Select cell containing the function to edit.

NOTE: Do not double-click the cell.

2 Click the **Paste Function** button on Standard toolbar.

3 Change arguments in **Number** boxes as desired, then click **OK**.

Notes:

- For this procedure, refer to illustrations on the previous page.

- A **nested function** is a function that contains a function as an argument.

Combine (Nest) Functions

1 Double-click cell containing function(s).

2 Place insertion point where new function will be inserted, or select argument to replace with a function.

3 Click the **Paste Function** button on Standard toolbar.

4 Select desired category in **Function category.**

5 Select desired function in **Function name** list, then click **OK**.

6 Insert cell references or values in **Number** boxes that appear.

7 Click **OK** when done.

=AVERAGE(B5:B9,SUM(B6:D6))

Nested Functions

Notes:

- If Excel detects subtotals within a range of values, it may suggest to add just those totals to obtain a grand total. When this happens, Excel applies dashed outlines only to the cells containing subtotals in the immediate column or row.

Use AutoSum Function

1 Click cell to receive the function.

2 Click **AutoSum** button on Standard toolbar [Σ].

Excel suggests cells to add with dashed outline.

3 To change the proposed range, drag through desired cells.

4 Press **Enter** when done.

	A	B	C	D	E
4		ELMHURST	CADDY	TOTALS	
5	SALES	640000	340000	=SUM(B5:C5)	
6	BONUS	2000	1000		

Edit Formulas

You will sometimes need to change a formula — perhaps replace an operator, add a set of parentheses, or change a cell or range the formula refers to.

Notes:

- After you double-click the cell, Excel displays the formula in the cell and on the formula bar.

- To insert a function, click desired location in formula, or select function name to replace, then click the **Functions** button to the right of the formula bar (it shows the last function selected), then follow the prompts to complete the function.

- If the result achieved by editing the formula is incorrect, you can click **Edit** menu, then **Undo Typing** to undo your change.

Edit Formulas

1 Double-click the cell containing the formula to change.

Excel displays a flashing insertion pointer in the formula indicating where changes will be made. Cell references in the formula are colored, and cell outlines indicate locations of references in worksheet.

AVERAGE	▼	X ✓ =	=SUM(C4:C9)

editcalcs.xls

	A	B	C	
2			Sales	Exp
3		1991	35000	
4		1992	40000	
5		1993	300000	
6		1994	35000	
7		1995	39000	
8		1996	43000	
9				
10		Totals	=SUM(C4:C9)	
11				

2 Click in the entry to place the insertion pointer.

OR

Drag through characters to select (next action will replace or delete your selection) .

3 Edit the entry as needed:

- Type characters to insert.

- Press **Del** to delete characters to the right of insertion pointer or to delete the selection.

- Press **Backspace** to delete characters to the left of the insertion pointer or to delete the selection.

- Follow steps described on the next page to change reference or extend a cell range.

4 Press **Enter** or click ✓ on formula bar.

OR

To cancel the change:

Press **Esc**, or click ✗ on formula bar.

Notes:

- Excel assigns a color to each border and reference to help you identify them.

Change Reference in Formula

1 Double-click the formula to change.

Excel outlines references in worksheet with colored borders.

2 Point to border of outlined reference in worksheet.

Pointer becomes an arrow when positioned correctly.

3 Drag outline to desired cell or range.

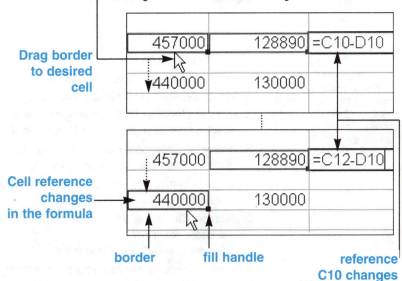

Drag border to desired cell

457000	128890	=C10-D10
440000	130000	

Cell reference changes in the formula

457000	128890	=C12-D10
440000	130000	

border   **fill handle**   **reference C10 changes to C12**

Notes:

- In **step 2**, Excel changes pointer to a crosshair to indicate that you can drag it to extend the range.

Extend Cell Range in Formula

1 Double-click the formula to change.

Excel outlines references in worksheet with colored borders.

2 Point to fill handle of outlined reference in worksheet.

Pointer becomes a crosshair when positioned correctly.

3 Drag fill handle in direction to extend the range.

40000	20000
300000	15000
35000	33000
39000	25890
43000	35000

=SUM(C4:C8)

40000	20000
300000	15000
35000	33000
39000	25890
43000	35000

=SUM(C4:D8)

Range C4:C8 becomes . . .   **C4:D8**

Print Workbook Data

The Print feature lets you print the current worksheet, a selection in a worksheet, or an entire workbook. Additionally, you can specify which pages to print, collate printed pages, print multiple copies, and print to a file.

Print button

Notes:

• Consider using **Print Preview** to check just how the worksheet will print prior to printing it *(see Print Preview)*.

Settings that Affect Print Results

Before printing a worksheet or workbook, consider this checklist of settings that will affect the print results:

Headers and footers: Prints repeating information at the top and bottom of each page. *(See Headers and Footers.)*

Page breaks: Determines locations in worksheet where printed pages end and new pages start. *(See Page Breaks.)*

Margins: Determines free space around printed page. *(See Set Margins.)*

Orientation: Determines whether the page prints in a portrait or landscape orientation. *(See Set Scale and Page Orientation.)*

Print area: Prints a specified area of the worksheet. *(See Set Print Area.)*

Repeating print titles: Prints column titles at the top or left side of each new printed page. *(See Repeating Print Titles.)*

Scale: Determines the size of the worksheet information will be when printed. *(See Set Scale and Page Orientation.)*

Sheet options: Sets print options, such as gridlines, page order, draft quality, black and white printing. *(See Set Sheet Print Options.)*

Notes:

• Consider using **Print Preview** to check just how the worksheet will print prior to printing it *(see Print Preview)*.

Print Using Toolbar

1 Select worksheets, worksheet cells, or chart object to print.

OR

Select any cell to print current worksheet.

2 Click **Print** button on Standard toolbar.

Print Using Menu

1 Select worksheets, worksheet cells, or chart object to print.
OR
Select any cell to print current worksheet.

2 Click **File** menu, then click **Print**.
The Print dialog box appears.

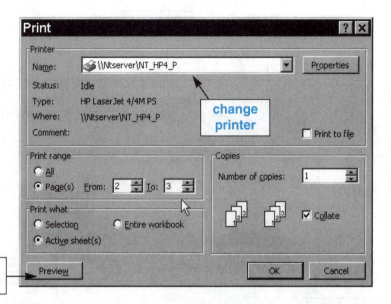

change printer

click to preview

To indicate what to print:

• Select **Selection**, **Entire workbook**, or **Active sheet(s)**.

To specify pages to print:

• Select **All**, or select pages to print in **From** and **To** boxes.

To disable collating of printed pages:

• Deselect **Collate**.

To print multiple copies:

• Select number of copies in **Number of copies** box.

To print to a file:

• Select **Print to file**.

3 Click **OK** to print.

About Chart Items

When you create and modify charts, you will be presented with many choices and settings. Understanding the items that make up a chart and their properties will make it easier for you to make decisions and to know what is possible.

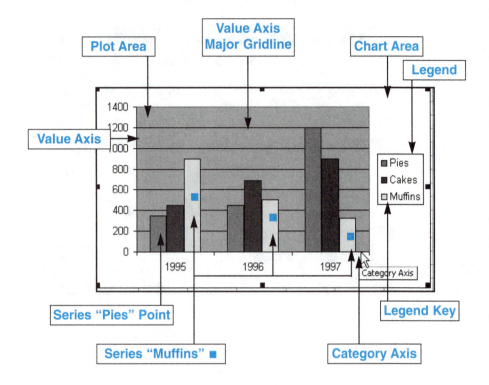

Items in Default Clustered Column Chart

Notes:

- When you rest the pointer on any chart item, Excel displays a pop-up label identifying the name of the item, as shown in the illustration (Category Axis) above.

Identify Chart Items

The default Clustered Column chart type shown above is made up of the items described below. Each item contains properties which are briefly described as well.

Category Axis (X Axis) — the horizontal line on which categories of data are usually plotted. The properties of this item include the format and alignment of category names and the scale of names and tick marks.

Chart Area — the space inside the chart that includes the base properties of all items in the chart, such as font style for chart text, background color, and how the chart moves or sizes when cells around it change.

- To review the properties of any chart item, rest the pointer on the item. When Excel displays the item name, double-click to display the Format dialog box for the item.

- Charts of different types have items or properties unique to their type. For example, pie charts have properties for a series that describes the angle of the first slice, while line charts have properties such as drop lines and up-down bars.

Legend — a box containing a label and legend key for each series in the chart. Properties of a legend include its border, font, and placement.

Legend Key — a graphic in the legend whose color or pattern corresponds to a series in the chart. Legend key properties include border, color, shadow, and fill effects.

Plot Area — the area within which the chart axes and series data is drawn. The properties of plot area include its border, area color, and fill effects.

Series — a group of data markers or series points that visually describe the values you have plotted. For example, the Series "Muffins" describes the number of muffins sold in each category (1995, 1996, and 1997). The properties of data series include borders and colors, plot axes, error bars, data labels, series order, and options such as overlap and gap width.

Series Point — a single item in a data series that visually describes the value for one category of a series. For example, Series "Pies" Point indicates a value of 345 for the category 1995. The properties for series points include border and pattern, data labels, and options such as overlap and gap width.

Value Axis (Y Axis) — the vertical line that describes the values of series points in the chart. The properties of the value axis include line and tick marks, scale of major and minor values, font for displayed values, number style of values, and alignment of values.

Value Axis Major Gridlines — a set of lines that visually defines values across the plot area. These gridlines make it easier to determine the value of a given series point in the chart. The properties of value axis gridlines include color, style, pattern, and units of values to display gridlines for.

Create a Chart

The Chart Wizard makes it easy to create a chart. It provides prompts and options for selecting the chart type, the source data, chart options, and chart location.

Chart Wizard button

Insert ➡ 📊 Chart...

Notes:

- The shape of your selection will determine the orientation of the series in your chart. You can change this orientation in **Chart Wizard - Step 2 of 4** in the **Data Range** tab.

- Avoid selecting blank rows and columns when selecting data to chart. You can use the **Ctrl** key and drag through ranges to create a multiple selection as a way to omit blank cells.

- You can hide rows and columns that do not pertain to data to be charted.

- From **Chart Wizard** steps, you can click **Next>** or **<Back** to move forward or backwards to any step.

- **Chart Wizard - Step 1 of 4:**

  First select the chart type, then the subtype. You should click and hold the **Press and hold to view sample** button to preview how your chart will be plotted

Create a Chart

1 Select cells containing labels and values to chart.

> *NOTE:* *You can change this selection as you proceed, if you discover that your selection is not what was required to chart the data properly.*

2 Click **Chart Wizard** button on Standard toolbar. 📊

From Chart Wizard - Step 1 of 4 - Chart Type:

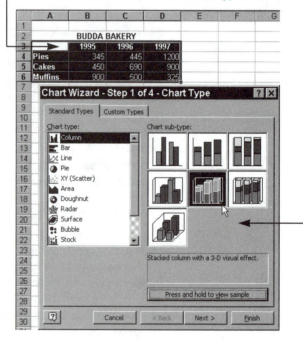

a Select chart type and subtype *(see Select Chart Type).*
b Click **Next >**.

From Chart Wizard - Step 2 of 4 - Chart Source Data:

- **Chart Wizard - Step 2 of 4:**

From the **Data Range** tab, you can change the range of data to plot, or change the orientation of the data series to either columns or rows.

From the **Series tab**, you can add and remove series and change references to series names, data ranges, and the category (X) axis labels.

- **Chart Wizard - Step 3 of 4:**

From the **Chart Options** dialog box, you can set options for chart titles, axes, gridlines, legend, data labels, and data table. You can go back to this dialog box after you've created the chart *(see Set Chart Options)*.

- **Chart Wizard - Step 4 of 4:**

From the **Chart Location** dialog box, you can change the proposed destination sheet, or change the proposed chart sheet name.

You can click **Finish** from any **Chart Wizard** step to quickly create the chart using default options.

From Chart Wizard - Step 2 of 4 - Chart Source Data:

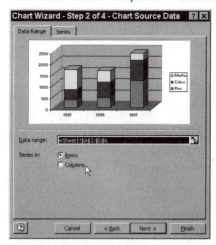

a   Select **Data Range** and **Series** option.

b   Click **Next >**.

From Chart Wizard - Step 3 of 4 - Chart Options:

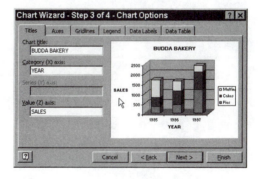

a   Select desired **Chart** options *(See Set Chart Options)*.

b   Click **Next >**.

From Chart Wizard - Step 4 of 4 - Chart Location:

a   Select **As new sheet** or **As object in**.

b   Click **Finish**.

109

Access

Microsoft Office's database application.
It is designed to create tables, forms and
reports based on records that you create.
Access helps organize this information, and
to use it as the basis of queries or searches,
which filter the data in specified ways.
Access helps you to manage large amounts
of information and to show relationships
among records. Like all other Microsoft
Office applications, Access also allows you to
arrange your data in visually attractive formats.

Create a Database

A database created from a template includes many predefined fields, or you can create a blank database manually.

Notes:

- Once you have created a database using a template, you can customize it as desired. To add fields see **Edit a Table** to customize forms and reports, see **Edit a Form or Report**.

Template

1 On the toolbar, click New button [ ] to open the New dialog box.

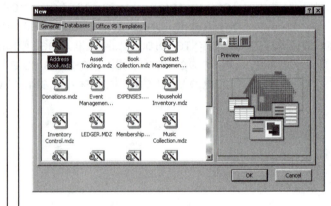

2 Click the Databases tab to bring it to the front.

3 Click desired database template.

4 Click [OK] to open the File New Database dialog box.

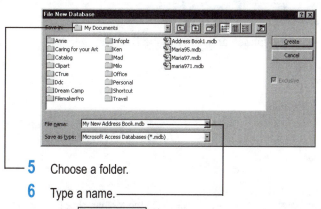

5 Choose a folder.

6 Type a name.

7 Click [Create].

8 Follow on-screen instructions.

Blank Database

[File] ➡ [New Database...]

1 On the toolbar, click New button 📄 to open the New dialog box.

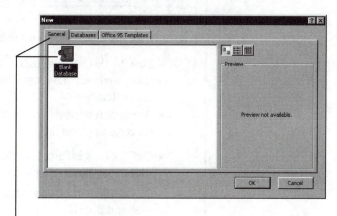

2 On the General tab, click Blank Database.

3 Click [OK] to open the File New Database dialog box.

4 Choose a folder.

5 Type a name.

6 Click [Create].

113

Open a Database

Opens any database and displays the Database window.

1 On the toolbar, click the Open button 📂.

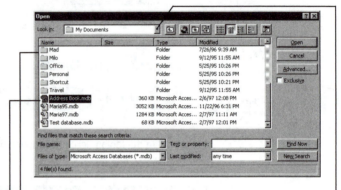

2 Choose the folder in which the database is stored:

• Click the Up One Level button ⬆ to display the folders stored along with the folder currently displayed in the Look in text box

• Double-click a folder icon in the list window to display the contents of that folder.

• Click the Look in Favorites button ⬆ to display favorite folders that you have chosen.

• Click the Look in drop-down button ▼ to choose another disk drive.

3 Choose how the list box displays your files:

• Click the List button ☷ to show as many files as possible.

• Click the Details button ▦ to show file information, such as size, type and date modified.

• Click the Properties button ▦ to show even more file information, including revision and printing history.

4 Click desired filename to open.

5 Click [Open].

Create a Table

Tables are the basic structural element of databases and they are used to store all the information about a particular subject.

1 Click the Tables tab in the database window.

2 Click New.

3 Click Datasheet View.

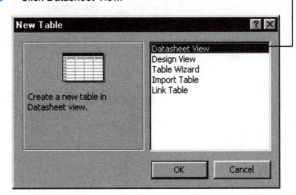

4 Click OK. (See **Edit a Table** to add fields to the table.)

115

Edit a Table

In a table's Design view, you can add or delete fields or change field properties.

Notes:

- It is best to create a field for each bit of data that you might want to use separately: first name, last name, street, city, state, postal code, country, for instance. This will allow you to print the information in any desired layout, as well as sort it by any desired field.

1 In the Database window, click the Tables tab to bring it to the front.

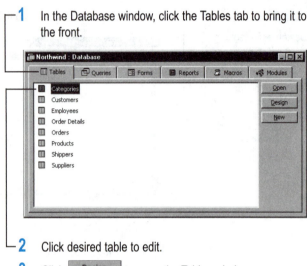

2 Click desired table to edit.

3 Click **Design** to open the Tables window.

• You can use Expression Builder to help you create expressions for certain Field properties.

4 Click an empty Field Name cell

OR

Click Insert Rows button 🗗 to create a new row between existing rows.

5 Type field name; press Tab to move to Data Type cell.

6 Click drop-down arrow and select a data type:

• Text – contains letters and numbers, up to 255 characters

• Memo – contains letters and numbers, up to 64,000 bytes

• Number – contains integers or fractional values

• Date/Time – contains date and time values

• Currency – contains monetary values

• AutoNumber – contains an automatically incremented numeric value

• Yes/No – contains Boolean values: yes/no, true/false, 0/-1.

• OLE object – contains graphic or binary data

• Hyperlink – contains a link to another location

• Lookup Wizard – creates a lookup column, which contains values found in another table or query, or entered by you (follow directions on screen).

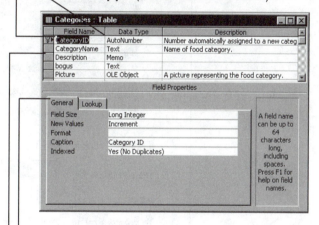

7 More specifics can be chosen in the Field Properties area, which will vary depending on the field type chosen. Point and click desired text box and set property as desired. More information on the property can be found in the information area to the right.

8 Click the Description cell and type any comments desired.

9 To delete a field and all its data, click the field row, then

click Delete Row 🗗 .

Define Relationships

Relationships allow Access to use related information from more than one table at a time.

Notes:

• Relationships may be one-to-one or one-to-many (a many-to-many relationship incorporates a one-to-many linking table).

1 Click Tools, Relationships to open the Relationships window.

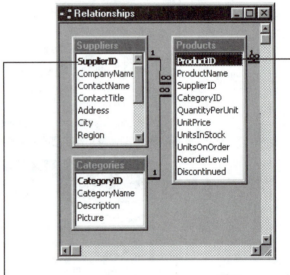

2 If needed, click the Add Table button and click desired table. Click Add . When finished adding tables, click Close .

3 To create a relationship, click any desired field in the primary table.

4 Drag the selected field and drop it on the related field in the secondary table. A second Relationships dialog box opens.

• Once table relationships are set, referential integrity can be enforced. This ensures that related data in another table will not be deleted.

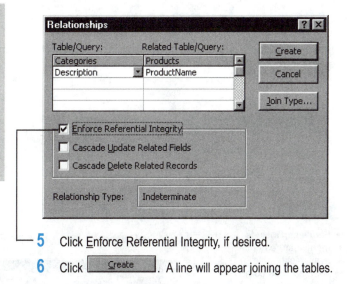

5 Click Enforce Referential Integrity, if desired.

6 Click [Create]. A line will appear joining the tables.

Create a Form

Forms make adding and editing data easier. You can create a form using a Wizard or create a form manually.

- Forms can include many features not available in table view, such as combo boxes, option buttons, check boxes and tab organizers.

Using a Wizard

1 In the Database window, click the Forms tab.

2 Click [New] to open the New Form dialog box.

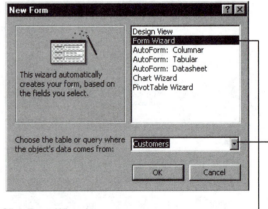

3 Click Form Wizard.

4 Click drop-down button and choose a table or query.

5 Click [OK].

6 Follow on-screen instructions.

Create a Blank Form

1 In the Database window, click the Forms tab.

2 Click **New** to open the New Form dialog box.

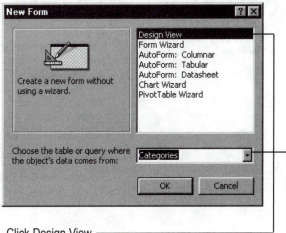

3 Click Design View.

4 Click the drop-down button to choose a table or query.

5 Click **OK**. (See **Edit Forms and Reports**.)

Enter Data

Information can be typed into a table, form or datasheet (see View Data, below).

Form or Datasheet

1 In the database window, click the Forms tab.

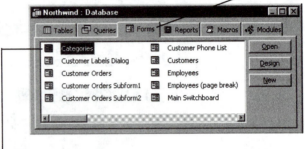

2 Click form to open.

3 Click [Open].

4 To view Datasheet, click the View drop-down button, then click Datasheet View.

5 Type data, pressing Tab or pointing and clicking to move from field to field.

Table

1 In database window, click Tables tab.

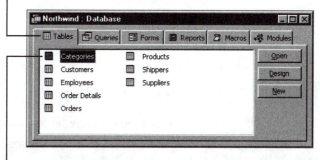

2 Click table to open.

3 Click [Open].

4 Type data, pressing Tab or pointing and clicking to move between fields.

New Record

On the toolbar, click the New Record button [image].

Delete Record

1 Click record's selector.

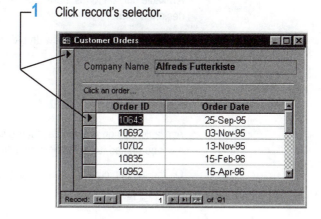

2 Press Delete.

3 Click Yes to confirm the deletion.

View Data

Forms, tables, reports and queries can be viewed in more than one way.

Notes:

• Form View and Datasheet View are the most commonly used for data entry.

Design View

Allows you to change the design and structure.

On the toolbar, click the <u>V</u>iew drop-down button and choose [Design View].

Datasheet View

Shows you records in column and row format.

On the toolbar, click the View drop-down button and click .

Form View

Available only on forms, Form View shows records in a specially designed form.

On the toolbar, click the View drop-down button and click [Form View].

Layout Preview

Available only on reports, Layout Preview displays a report as it will be printed, using sample data drawn from the database.

On the toolbar, click the View drop-down button and click 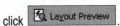.

Print Preview

Available only on reports, Print Preview displays a report as it will be printed, using real data.

On the toolbar, click the View drop-down button and click [Print Preview].

Continue

➡️

Format a Datasheet

Data displayed in column and row format can be changed and customized in a number of ways. The changes can be saved with the Datasheet.

Notes:

- You can print an on-the-fly report based on your datasheet design. Filter the records desired (see **Filter Data**), format the datasheet, and click the Print button.

Change Column and Row Size

1 To change column size, click right edge of column label and drag to desired size (the other columns will move to fit).

2 To automatically fit column size to data, double-click the right edge of the column label.

3 To change row size, click bottom edge of record selector and drag to desired size (all rows will change size).

Move Columns

1 Click and drag over column labels to select columns to move.

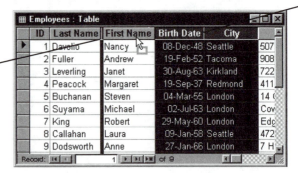

2 Click and drag selector to the new location (existing columns will move to the right).

126

Notes:

Format Cells and Gridlines

• You can change the
  size of an entire
  column or row, but
  not of a single cell.

1 Click Format, Cells to open the Cell Effects dialog box.

2 To change display of gridlines, click Gridlines Shown checkboxes.

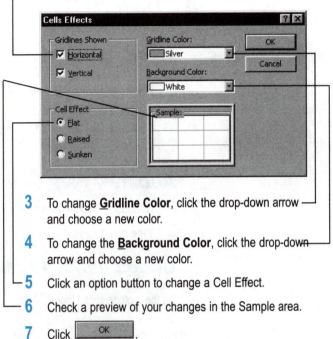

3 To change **Gridline Color**, click the drop-down arrow and choose a new color.

4 To change the **Background Color**, click the drop-down arrow and choose a new color.

5 Click an option button to change a Cell Effect.

6 Check a preview of your changes in the Sample area.

7 Click ☐ OK ☐.

Edit Data

Access automatically saves changes to a field when you move to the next record.

Notes:

• You can move to a cell by clicking on the desired cell or using navigation commands (see next page).

Replace data in field

1 Press Tab to move to field and select all data.

OR

Click and drag across data to replace.

2 Type desired new value.

Add new data to field

1 Click desired location in field to change.

2 Type data to add.

Undo changes to field data

On the toolbar, click Undo 🔙 .

OR

Press Escape while still in the field.

Undo changes to record data

On the toolbar, repeatedly click Undo 🔙 .

OR

Press Escape while still in the record.

Navigate Records and Fields

Next field or next record	Tab or down arrow
Previous field or previous record	Shift + tab or up arrow
First field of row	Home
Last field of row	End
Next record, Form view	▣ or ctrl + page down
Previous record, Form view	�«▣ or ctrl + page up
Next record, Datasheet view	Down arrow
Previous record, Datasheet view	Up arrow
First record, Form View	◄▣
Last record, Form View	▶▣
Next form section	F6
Open combo box, form view	Alt + down arrow
Open Zoom box	Shift + F2

Keystrokes for editing

Insert line return in field	Ctrl + enter
Duplicate field value from previous record	Ctrl + single quote
Save changes	Shift + enter
Requery records	Shift + F9

129

Copy and Move Data

In Access you can copy or move the contents of a single field, a group of fields or selected fields from a group of records.

Copy data to another field

1 In Form View or Datasheet View, highlight data to copy. (click immediately to the left of the data you want to copy). You can select data in a cell, several cells, or, by dragging over labels or selectors, several records or columns.

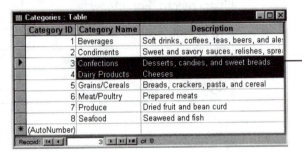

2 On the toolbar, click the Copy button ▣.

3 Highlight fields to receive copied data.

4 On the toolbar, click the Paste button ▣.

130

Move data to another field

1 In Form View or Datasheet View, select data to move (you can cut data within a single field or, by dragging the record selectors, entire records).

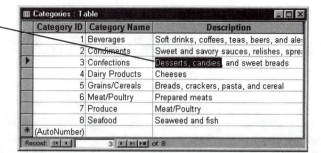

2 On the toolbar, click the Cut button.

3 Select data in field to be replaced by copied data.

4 On the toolbar, click the Paste button.

131

Find Data

Use Find to look up specific records one at a time.

Notes:

• Use wildcards in the Find What text box to increase your search power: * stands for any number of characters, ? stands for any single character, # stands for any single number.

1 Click field that contains information to look for.

2 On the toolbar, click the Find button 🔍 .

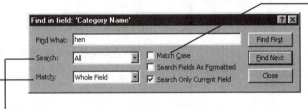

3 In the Find What text box, type the information to look for.

4 Click the Search drop-down and specify which records to search:

• All—finds the information if it appears in any record

• Up—looks for the information in previous records

• Down—looks for the information in the following records.

5 Click the Match drop-down and specify the type of match:

• Whole Field—find fields containing *only* the Find What text.

• Any Part of Field—finds fields that contain the Find What text anywhere in the field.

• Start of Field—finds fields that begin with the Find What text.

6 Click additional options as desired:———

• **Match Case**—finds only fields that match the capitalization of the Find What text.

• **Search Fields As Formatted**—used mostly for date and time fields; clearing it searches fields based on their value.

• **Search only Current Field**—when this option is cleared, all fields in database will be searched.

7   Click [Find Next] to begin search at current record

OR

Click [Find First] to begin search at first record of found set.

8   Click [Find Next] to move to next instance of matching text.

9   When finished, click [Close].

Filter Data

Finds a group of records with information that matches your specifications. Currently used filters are saved when you save the form.

Notes:

• Don't be surprised when Access adds proper code to your criteria in the Filter by Form window.

Filter by selection

Finds records matching data you select.

1 In Form or Datasheet View highlight data to match.

2 On the toolbar, click the Filter by Selection button .

3 To further filter records, repeat steps 1 and 2.

4 To view all records, click the Remove/Apply Filter button .

Filter by form

Finds records based on data typed into the filtering form. Also finds records based on criteria from more than one field.

1 In Form or Datasheet View, click the Filter by Form button.

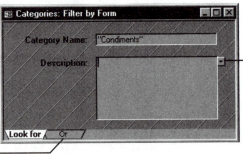

2 Click a field, then click its drop-down button to select criteria

OR

Click a field and type criteria to match.

(Repeatedly click a checkbox to cycle through filter possibilities: yes, no or not used.)

3 Click the **Or** tab to specify more fields to include.

4 Click the Apply Filter button.

134

Clear filter

1 Click the Filter by Form button 🔳.

2 Click the Delete button ✕.

3 Click **Close** to return to previous screen.

Save a filter

Saves and names a filter, which appears on the Query tab of the Database window.

1 While viewing desired filtered records, click the

Filter by Form button 🔳.

2 Click Save as Query button 💾.

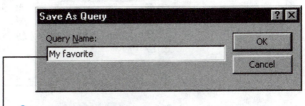

3 Type a Query Name in the text box.

4 Click ___OK___ .

3 Click **Close** to return to filtered search.

Load a saved filter

1 Click the Filter by Form button 🔳.

2 Click the Load from Query button 📂.

3 Select desired filter; click ___OK___ .

4 Click Apply Filter button 🔽.

Create a Query

A query displays specified records and fields from one or more tables in Datasheet View.

Notes:

• Find more ways to express query criteria by looking up "criteria" in the Help index.

Using a Wizard

1 In the Database window, click the Query tab.

2 Click [New].

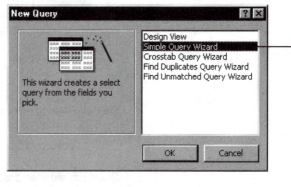

3 Click desired Wizard selection; note description at left.

4 Click [OK]. Follow on-screen instructions.

Design a query

1 In the Database window, click the Query tab.

2 Click ⎿ New ⏋.

3 Click Design View and click ⎿ OK ⏋.

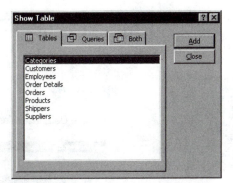

4 Click desired table to use and click ⎿ Add ⏋ button.

5 Repeat step 4 adding all tables and queries desired.

Click ⎿ Close ⏋.

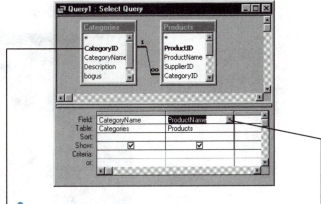

6 Click and drag fields to include from the field list to a Field cell in the lower part of the window.

OR

In the Field cell, click the drop-down arrow to choose a field.

OR

Click and drag the asterisk to the Field cell to include all fields in the field list.

7 Click the Save button 🖫 ; type a query name; click **OK**.

8 To view the query record set, click the Datasheet View button 🎛 .

Create a Report

Design reports to print information from your database. You can create a report using a Wizard for help, or you can create one manually.

Notes:

• You can customize a report created with a wizard; see **Edit a Form or Report**.

Wizard

1 In the Database window, click the Report tab.

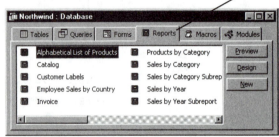

2 Click the New button.

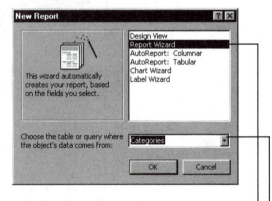

3 Click Report Wizard, Chart Wizard or Label Wizard.

4 Click the drop-down and choose a table or query on which to base the report.

5 Click OK.

6 Follow on-screen instructions.

138

Manual

1 In the Database window, click the Report tab.

2 Click the [New] button.

3 Click Design View.

4 Click the drop-down and choose a table or category on which to base the report.

5 Click [OK]. (See **Edit Forms and Reports** to add fields.)

Print a Report

You can print reports using a variety of settings for page orientation and margins, for example, and you can preview a report before you print it.

Notes:

- If you like, you can output a report to Word for further tweaking: in the Preview window, click the Word button.

Preview Report

1 In the Database window, click the Report tab.

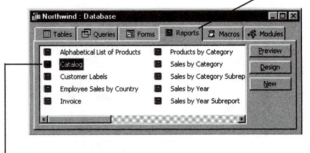

2 Click report to preview.

3 Click the Preview button.

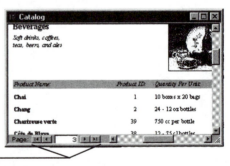

4 Click navigation buttons to view different pages:
- First page
- Previous page
- Next page
- Last page.

5 Click the Zoom button 🔍 to view a close up or full-page.

6 Click the Zoom drop-down button 75% ▾ to view the page at a specific scale.

7 Click the Multiple Pages button 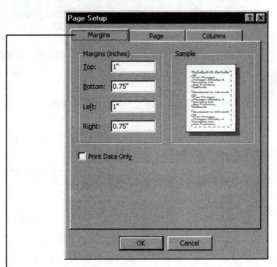 and drag to select number of pages to show on one screen.

8 To return to the Database window, click Close .

OR

Click the Design View button ▧ ▾ to see the report in design view.

Print

1 In the Database window, click the Reports tab, then click desired report.

OR

View desired report in Print Preview.

2 On the toolbar, click the Print button 🖨 .

Change Printer Settings

1 View desired report in Print Preview or Design View (see above).

2 Click File, Page Setup to open the Page Setup dialog.

3 Click tab for desired setting to change and adjust as desired.

4 Click OK when finished.

Notes:

- Use the Page Setup dialog box to set margins, paper orientation, columns, and paper size and source. The settings will be saved with the report.

141

Edit a Form or Report

Form and Report layouts can be changed and customized by placing a variety of controls on the layout.

Add a Control

1 View the form or report to edit in Design view.

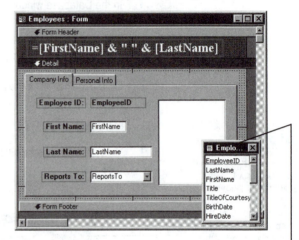

2 To display a field list, on the toolbar, click the Field List button ⊞.

3 Click on Toolbox 🛠.

4 To add a field, click tool for desired field type:

- Text field **abl** — to display alphanumeric data in an ordinary field

- Check box ☑ — to display yes/no data as a checkbox

- Combo box 🔲 — to allow the user to enter data by choosing from a drop-down list or by typing

- List box 🔳 — to force the user to choose data from a list

- Bound Object frame 🖼 — to contain an image, recording or other OLE object.

5   Click the Control Wizard button .

6   Click and drag desired field from the field list window to desired location on the layout.

7   To add other design elements, click toolbar to add:

   • Label *Aa* — to add text

   • Image 🖼 — to add clip art or another image

   • Page break — to cause a break to the next page or screen

   • Line ＼ — to add a line

   • Rectangle ▢ — to add a rectangle.

8   Click layout at desired location. Drag to draw a label box, line, or rectangle.

Move a Control

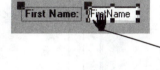

1   Click the control to select it (handles will appear at the corners and edges).

2   Point to a blank edge of the control (the pointer appears as a hand).

3   Drag the control to the new location.

Resize a Control

1   To change the size of a field or other control, click the control to select it.

2   Click and drag a handle to desired new size.

Delete a Control

1   Click the control to select it.

2   Press Del. (Deleting a control does not delete table data.)

Change Layout Size

Click and drag the bottom or right edge of the section.

Save Form or Report

Click the Save button 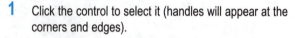.

Properties

Many of the objects, elements, and controls of Access have Properties settings that you can customize. Properties control additional aspects of objects that are not set using menus or toolbars.

Form or Report Control Properties

1 In Design view, click the object and, on the toolbar, click

the Properties button 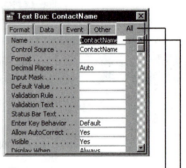 to display the Properties Sheet.

OR

Double-click the object.

2 Click desired tab to bring it to the front.

3 Change properties as desired (see below).

Property	Use
Caption	Contains text for column, form or report labels. Otherwise, the field name is used.
Decimal places	Determines the number of decimal places displayed for number fields.
Default value	Specifies a value automatically assigned to the field.
Format	Determines the display of data, such as the associated symbols with number fields, the translation of yes/no data, and the wording of date/time data.
Required	Determines whether data is required to be inputted into the field.
Can Grow	For printouts, allows field to enlarge to show all data.
Can shrink	For printouts, allows field to shrink around data to close up empty space.
Font name	Specifies font.
Font size	Specifies font size.

Form and Report Properties

1   In Design view, click an area in the Form or Report window outside the form or report layout.

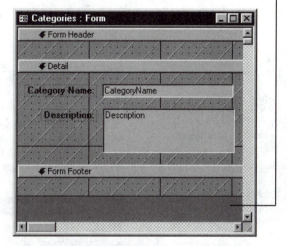

2   On the toolbar, click the Properties button to display the Properties Sheet.

3   Change properties as desired.

Property	Use
Record Source	Specifies table or query from which displayed records are drawn.
Default View	Specifies whether Form or Datasheet view will be displayed on opening.
Views Allowed	Limits view to Form or Datasheet.
Allow Edits/Deletions/Additions	Controls data entry.

Expressions

Expressions are used in queries, forms and reports to provide values calculated based on your formulas.

Notes:

- Expressions can be used to display the current date or page number, or to string field values.

- Expressions in Control Source tell Access where to get the data that will be displayed in the text box.

- In a form or report, you will have to create your own label for the text box containing the expression.

Enter Expression in a Control on a Form or Report

1 Click an unbound text field to contain the expression (see **Edit a Form**).

2 Click the Properties button [icon] (see **Properties**).

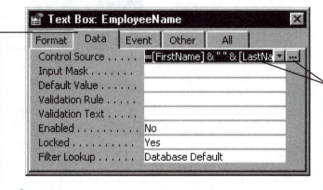

3 Click the Data tab and click the Control Source property.

4 Type = and desired expression.

OR

Press the Build button to open the Expression Builder to construct expression.

Enter Expression in Query

1 In Database window, click the Query tab.

2 Click query to view and click [Design].

Notes:

- The name you type before the colon becomes the field label.

- Equal signs do **not** precede expressions in queries.

3 Click an empty field cell to use for expression.

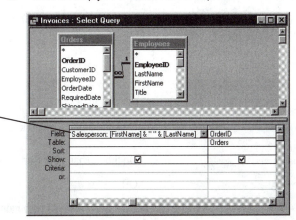

4 Type a name for the expression followed by a colon.

5 Type desired expression

OR

On the toolbar, click the Build button 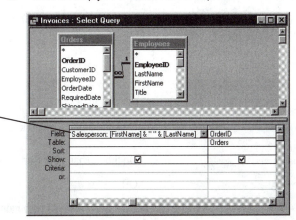 to open the Expression Builder.

Expressions and Examples

When using a field name in an expression, surround it with square brackets. When using text, surround it with quotations. (In the first example below, the space is enclosed in quotation marks so that the fields don't run together.)

Operator	Use	Example	Sample Result
&	Strings text	[first name] & " " & [last name]	Jun Smit
Chr$10 & Chr$13	Inserts a line return	[first name] & " " & [last name] & Chr$10 & Chr$13 & [company name]	Jun Smit Ajax Company
Date()	Current date	=Date	January 24, 1998
Page()	Current page	="page " & page()	page 53
*	Multiplies	=[rate]*[hours]	(20 * 5=) 100
-	Subtracts	=[rate]-5	(20-5=) 15
+	Adds	=[rate]+5	(20+5=) 25
/	Divides	=[rate]/5	(20/5=) 4

Sort Data

A sort order is a type of filter and is saved when the form is saved. To sort by more than one field, see **Query**.

1 Click the field by which to sort the records.

2 On the toolbar, click Sort Ascending button 🔼.

OR

Click Sort Descending button 🔽.

PowerPoint

Microsoft Office's presentation application that helps you to create interactive, self-running, or speaker-controlled visual displays. PowerPoint makes use of multimedia technology to include photographs, drawings, text, graphs, video and audio clips in your presentation. Presentations created in PowerPoint can be used to accompany lectures or as the basis for Web sites. PowerPoint can also be used to create 35-millimeter slides, overhead projections, and printed handouts.

Animation

Animation controls when and how slide components appear on screen.

Notes:

- Animation will only be seen if you are running a Slide Show.

- Animation can be set to run automatically, or manually.

- In earlier versions of PowerPoint, the animations were referred to as builds.

- Choose **Slide Show/ Preset Animation** to see a list of commonly used effects.

- Animation can only be seen during slide show.

The Custom Animation dialog box controls the order of the objects in a build:

1 Click **Custom Animation** from the **Slide Show** menu.

2 To **Start Animation**, select the **Animate** option button.

3 The ‾Animation order‾ box lists the order in which each object will be shown on the screen.

4 The arrows ⬆⬇ move the selected object up or down in the Animation order list box.

5 A thumbnail view of the slide is shown. ⟋

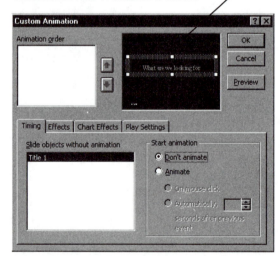

4 Click ‾OK‾ to apply the animation settings to the slide.
OR

Click ‾Cancel‾ to return to the presentation without making any changes.

OR

Click ‾Preview‾ to see what the slide will look like with the animations running.

Effects Tab

1 The **Effects** drop-down list [No Effect] allows you to view the various animation options that are available.

Note: Animation effects include text flying in from the right of the screen, for example, or appearing one letter at a time (typewriter effect). Options will depend on the system.

2 The **Sound** drop-down list [No Sound] allows you to view the various sound effect options that are available.

Note: Sounds might include screeching brakes or a swoosh, depending on the system.

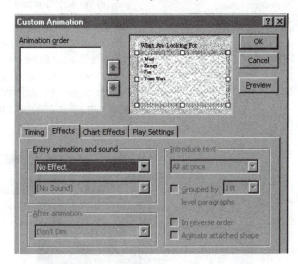

3 Once an object has been introduced to the screen and discussed, you may want to dim it out as the next point is brought to the screen. The **After Animation** drop-down list [Don't Dim] shows a number of options to de-emphasize an object once the next one has moved into its place.

4 Objects other than text can be animated, including shapes, using [Animate attached shape].

5 [In reverse order] causes objects to appear in reverse order, from the bottom to the top.

6 Choose the levels of text that you would like to appear on each build. If there are various paragraph levels, they can be built from the lowest to the highest, or vice-versa.

151

AutoContent Wizard

The AutoContent Wizard steps you through a series of questions and then formats a presentation based on your decisions.

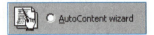

Notes:

- The AutoContent Wizard can help "jump start" a presentation by providing a skeleton to be filled in.

1 The AutoContent Wizard can be accessed from the opening dialog box, or by clicking **File**, **New** and double-clicking the **AutoContent Wizard** on the Presentations tab.

2 The left side of the screen shows you what step you are on in creating the presentation, while the right side contains choices to be made regarding the presentation. These choices include what type of information is to be presented, how PowerPoint will output the slides and what formatting options to use.

3 Click <u>Next ></u> to advance to the next screen of the Wizard.

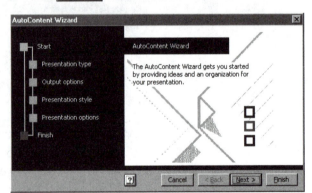

4 Click < <u>Back</u> to return to the previous screen in the Wizard.

5 Click <u>Finish</u> to complete the presentation immediately, accepting defaults where decisions have not been made.

6 If necessary, click 🔲 to activate the Office Assistant.

7 Click <u>Cancel</u> to exit the Wizard without creating a new presentation.

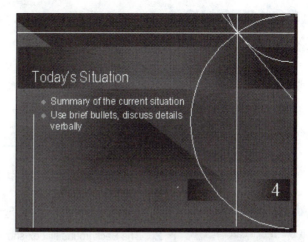

8 Once the Wizard has been completed, a presentation will be created based on the decisions you made.

Background

Colors and textures on the background of each slide can be formatted.

Notes:

- PowerPoint can set a background texture for a presentation.

- Backgrounds can add depth to a presentation.

1 Click **Background** on the **Format** menu.

2 The Background fill box shows a preview of how your slide(s) will look with a particular fill. The preview shows how screen objects, as well as the background, will look.

3 To select a background texture, click the drop-down arrow next to the lower box ▨▨▨▨▨ and select **Fill Effects**. Then click on the Texture tab. Available textures vary from system to system and may include such choices as pebbled or marble. To choose a variegated effect, click on the Gradient tab.

4 Click Preview to see what the slide will look like with the selected background.

5 Choosing ☐ Omit background graphics from master keeps the formatting that you select from being entered on the Master slide.

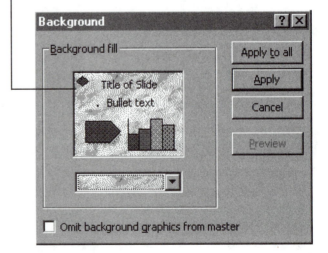

5 Click [Apply to all] to apply the background settings to the entire presentation.
OR

Click [Apply] to apply the background settings to the selected slide or slides.
OR

Click [Cancel] to return PowerPoint to the presentation without making any changes.

No Background

Granite Background

Clip Art

Clip Art adds visual interest and emotional impact to slides.

Insert ➡ Picture ▸ ➡ 🖼 Clip Art...

1 When you click **Insert**, **Picture**, **Clip Art**, the Microsoft Clip Gallery dialog box opens with the Clip Art tab selected. On the left of the tab is a listing of categories. Highlight the one that most closely fits your needs. Some images may appear in more than one category.

2 The available images for each category are displayed in the center of each tab. View the images in the category you selected; if you see an image you want to use in your presentation, select it by clicking on it.

3 The ☐ Magnify feature magnifies the selected image for better viewing.

4 If you do not see an image you like, you can try viewing other categories, or click Find... . **Find** searches for clipart based on a number of criteria, including the keywords displayed at the bottom of the screen.

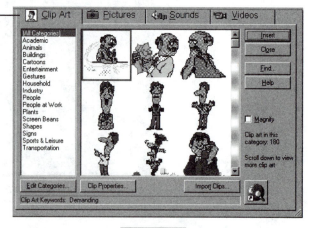

5 If necessary, click Help to access the Office Assistant.

6 Once you have selected the image you want to use, click Insert .

Notes:

- ClipArt is most easily positioned by changing the Slide Layout to Text & Clip Art or Clip Art's text.

- Double-click on the Clip Art placeholder to Open the Clip Gallery.

Additional Information About Clip Art:

- You can bring clipart from other applications, such as a graphics program, into the Clip Gallery using the [Import Clips...] button.

- Information about each clip, including the keyword(s) assigned to it and the categories it belongs in, can be displayed and edited using the [Clip Properties...] button. The Clip Properties dialog box will also open automatically when you import clipart.

- The [Edit Categories...] button opens a dialog box in which categories can be added, deleted, or renamed.

Color Schemes

Color Schemes are collections of color settings for objects on slides.

Notes:

- The use of Color Schemes allows for consistency in color throughout a presentation.

- Colors applied to individual objects before you apply a Color Scheme may be overridden.

- Colors of specific objects can be easily adjusted after a Color Scheme has been applied.

- You can also delete a color scheme using

  [Delete Scheme]

  This will permanently remove it from the dialog box for all presentations. Once a color scheme is deleted, the procedure cannot be undone.

When you click **Format**, **Slide Color Scheme**, a dialog box opens, displaying various options. You can choose a predesigned color scheme from the standard tab or create your own scheme on the custom tab.

Standard Tab

1   Click on any one of the provided **Color Schemes** to select it. An outline appears around the selected scheme.

2   Click [Preview] to see a preview of your slide with the Color Scheme applied.

3   Click [Apply to All] to apply the color scheme to the entire presentation.

    OR

    Click [Apply] to apply the scheme to just the slide or slides that were selected before accessing the Color Scheme dialog box.

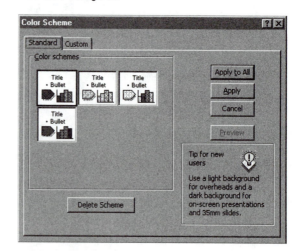

    OR

    Click [Cancel] to return to the presentation without making any changes.

Custom Tab

1 The Custom tab displays a list of slide objects and their currently set colors. To change the color of an object, click on the box to the left of its name (an outline will appear around the box) and then click Change Color... .

2 A dialog box with two tabs will appear. The standard tab contains a color wheel from which you can choose a color for the selected object. The custom tab contains a color palette and boxes in which various color attributes can be set.

3 Click Preview to see a preview of your slides with the Color Scheme applied.

4 Click Apply to All to apply the color scheme to the entire presentation.

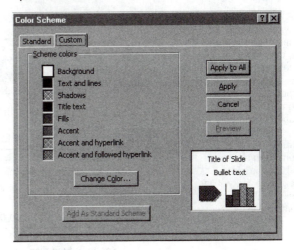

OR

Click Apply to apply the scheme to just the slide or slides that were selected before accessing the Color Scheme dialog box.

OR

Click Cancel to return to the presentation without making any changes.

5 Click on Add As Standard Scheme to add the newly created scheme to the list of Standard Color Schemes on the Standard tab. This will affect the Color Scheme dialog box for all presentations.

Find File

The Find File feature allows you to search a drive for a specific file, or for files that fit certain criteria.

Notes:

- If the File Properties feature has been filled in, advanced searches can be run.

- A Wildcard is a symbol used in a search to substitute for unknown characters. The asterisk (*) is used to indicate an unknown group of characters, and the question mark (?) is used to substitute for an unknown single character. For example, Br* will find all files that begin with the letters Br.

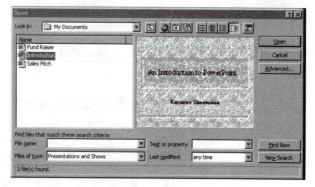

To find a file using options on the Open dialog box, you can:

1 Type the name of the file to be found in the File name: text box, or use wild-cards to set part of a name to be found. Use the drop-down list box to see a list of recently searched-for files.

2 Use the Files of type drop-down list box Files of type: Presentations and Shows to have only files of a specific type displayed.

3 Type any text that you know appears in the presentation in the Text or property: box, or choose a recently searched-for string of text from the drop-down list.

4 Choose a time frame in which the file or files were last saved from the Last modified: any time drop-down list. (You might not want to see files from earlier than last year, for example.)

5 Choose Find Now to run the search.

6 Choose New Search to clear all settings (including any Advanced Settings, below).

7 Click on Advanced... to go to the Advanced Search dialog box to try to find the file(s) using different settings.

Master Slide

A master slide acts as a pattern for all the slides in a presentation.
Any formatting applied to the master slide is applied to all slides in the presentation.

View ➡ Master ▶ ➡ Slide Master

Notes:

- Not *all* slides have to follow the Slide Master. For example, one slide may use a different background. To do this, select the slide to receive the new background, and click Apply, not Apply to All in the background dialog box.

1 When you select **View**, **Master**, **Slide Master**, the Slide Master will appear on the screen.

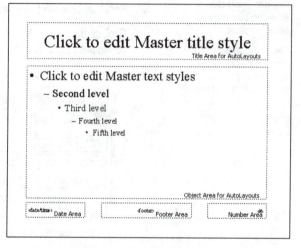

2 Click in the desired placeholders to change the font, font size, tabs, etc. You can also change the headers and footers.

3 You can apply a text color, background, color scheme, template, or any other decorative option to the Master Slide just as you would to a regular slide. Keep in mind, however, that all formats applied to the Master Slide apply to every slide in the presentation.

4 When you are done, click the **Master** box to exit out of the **Slide Master**.

New Slide

PowerPoint does not create new slides automatically; you must insert them.

1 Click **New Slide** on the **Insert** menu or click the **New Slide** icon 📑 on the Standard toolbar.

2 Scroll up or down to see available slide layouts.

3 Click on the desired layout in the **Choose an AutoLayout** box to select it. A dark border indicates the selected layout.

4 The name of the currently selected layout appears.

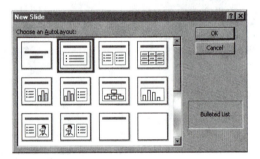

5 Click OK to insert a slide based on the selected layout.

OR

Click Cancel to return to the presentation without inserting a slide.

Notes Pages

Notes Pages are designed to be used by the speaker. They contain both the slide and the text of a speech.

Notes:

- Notes Pages are often used as Speaker's Notes for a presentation.

- To print Notes Pages, choose **Notes** in the **Print what** text box of the Print dialog box.

1 Click **Notes Pages** on the **View** menu or click the Notes Page View button 🖳 at the bottom left corner of your window.

2 Each slide in your presentation is shown at the top of the page. *Note: The slide cannot be edited in this view.*

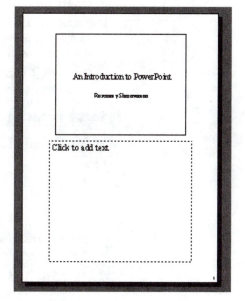

3 Click in the box below the slide to add notes.

4 Click a view button or select a different **View** to switch out of Notes Page view.

Open a Presentation

Opening a saved presentation is similar to opening any file in Windows.

Notes:

- The bottom of the **File** menu lists the last four files opened. If you want to open one of these, just click on its name.

1 Click **Open** on the **File** menu.

2 There are four buttons that control how files are displayed in the Open dialog box:

List lists the filenames in columns;

Details lists the filename as well as its size, type, and last modification date;

Properties displays the filename in the left-hand window and information from the file's Properties Sheet in the right-hand window.

Preview displays the filename in the left-hand window and a miniature of the slide in the right-hand window.

3 The Favorites folder is designed to hold often-used documents. Click to list files in the Favorites folder, or to add a selected file to the Favorites folder.

4 Use the Commands and Settings button to:

- **Sort** displayed files in a different manner (e.g., by type);
- **Print** a file.
- View its **Properties** without opening it.
- **Open Read-Only** copies of a file. If you select this option, the file will open, but no changes may be saved to it without specifying a different file name. This ensures that the original file saved in its original format.

164

5 Select the folder that contains the desired file in the Look in: [ ] My Documents ▼ drop-down list.

6 Click on the Up One Level button to move to the next highest folder.

7 Click the Search the Web button to search for a presentation on the Internet. (You must have a modem and a service provider to access this feature.)

8 Select the desired file from the list box.

9 Click Open to open the selected presentation.

OR

Click Cancel to exit the dialog box without opening a presentation.

Page Setup

Use the Page Setup dialog box to chose the size and orientation of the slides and notes pages.

Notes:

• Slides Orientation settings can be set separately from the Notes, Handouts, and Outline Settings.

1 Click **Page Setup** from the **File** menu.

2 Use the Slides sized for: drop-down list to have PowerPoint automatically size the slides for certain materials (letter paper, 35mm slides, etc.).

3 If you wish to use a material not listed, or if you wish to set the slides to a specific size, choose Custom from the drop-down list and type the desired Width: and Height: in the text boxes, or use the the increment arrows 1 to select the desired measurements.

3 Slide numbering will start with 1 unless you set a different number in the Number slides from: box.

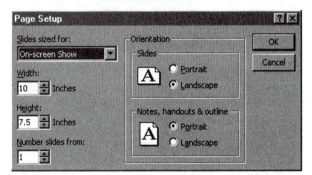

4 Choose from either **Portrait** (vertical) or **Landscape** (horizontal) orientation.

5 Click OK to return to the presentation and apply the settings.

OR

Click Cancel to return to the presentation without applying the settings.

Summary Slide

A summary slide can be created from a slide presentation. The title of each slide is extracted to create the summary slide.

1 In either Outline or Slide Sorter view, select the slides you wish to include in the summary. (Hold down Shift while clicking on each slide to select multiple slides.)

2 Click the summary slide icon 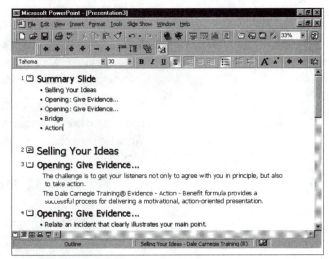. A slide containing the titles of all selected slides will appear in front of the first selected slide.

3 Each of the slides selected must contain text in the title placeholder for the summary function to be effective. Otherwise, the slide will be represented in the summary by a bullet that says "Topic [slide #]."

Set Up Show

The Set Up Show dialog box controls the way a Slide Show will run, whether control will be given to a view, and what slides will be shown.

Notes:

- Before you run a show, use PowerPoint's **Style Checker** on the **Tools** menu to check your slide's spelling, visual clarity (i.e., too many fonts), and inconsistencies in case and punctuation.

1 Click **Set Up Show** from the **Slide Show** menu.

2 Choose the Show type:

- ⦿ Presented by a speaker (full screen) a full-screen show directed by a speaker who controls the pacing, minutes and action items, hidden slides and other options.

- ○ Browsed by an individual (window) a presentation run in a custom, window, where the viewer controls how and how fast he or she goes through the presentation

- ○ Browsed at a kiosk (full screen) a self-running, full-screen presentation in which there is more automation and fewer options for the viewer).

3 Click ☐ Loop continuously until 'Esc' if you want the presentation to keep repeating until Esc is pressed. When the presentation reaches the last slide, it will loop back to the first.

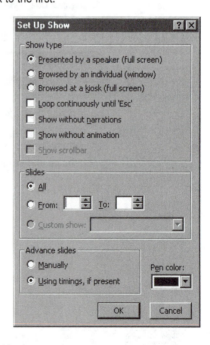

3 Click ☐ Show without narrations or ☐ Show without animation or both if you will be running the presentation on a system with limited resources.

4 Click ☐ Show scrollbar to let viewers manually advance a presentation. This option is automatically selected when you choose to have the presentation browsed by an individual.

5 Choose which Slide are to be shown:

⊙ All selects all slides.

○ From: ☐ ↕ To: ☐ ↕ allows you to select a range of consecutive slides;

○ Custom show: allows you to choose among custom shows you have created; the Custom Shows must already be set up for this option to be available.

6 If you check Advance Slides ○ Manually , the show will move to the next slide only when the mouse is clicked or Enter is pressed. If you want the slides to advance automatically, and you have set timings, check ⊙ Using timings, if present .

7 If the presentation will be **Presented by a speaker**, you can select a different Pen color: .

8 Click OK to accept the settings.

OR

Click Cancel to discard the settings and return to the presentation.

Transitions

Transitions are a way of moving from slide to slide in a Slide Show.

Slide Show ➡ Slide Transition...

Notes:

- In Slide Sorter view, an icon indicating that a transition has been applied will appear under the slide.

From Slide View or Outline View

1 Click **Slide Transition** on the **Slide Show** menu.

2 The **Effect** box contains a picture to demonstrate the transition effects before they are set.

3 Click the drop-down list `No Transition ▼` to select an effect.

4 Choose a speed by clicking the appropriate radio button.

5 Choose when the slide should make the transition: either **Automatically after** a set amount of time or **On mouse click**.

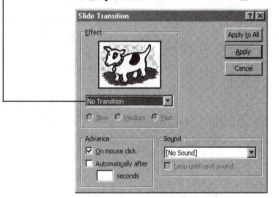

6 Click the `[No Sound] ▼` drop-down list box to apply a sound to the transition. The sound can only be heard if the computer running the Slide Show has the appropriate hardware.

7 Click `Apply to All` to apply the same transition to the entire presentation.

OR

Click `Apply` to apply the transition only to the selected slide(s).

OR

Click `Cancel` to return to the presentation without applying a transition.

170

From Slide Sorter View

1 In Slide Sorter view, the Formatting toolbar includes a transitioning icon . Click it and the **Slide Transition** dialog box will open.

2 You can also click on the transition drop-down list to select an effect. The Slide Transition dialog box will not open, however, so you cannot set timings from there.

Toolbars

In PowerPoint, different toolbars are available to assist you with various tasks. Toolbars are made up of buttons that quickly access various PowerPoint commands.

Notes:

- The Standard, Formatting, and Drawing toolbars display by default when you open PowerPoint.

COMMON TASKS TOOLBAR

The Common Tasks toolbar contains the most often used commands.

1 | New Slide... | Opens the New Slide dialog box.

2 | Slide Layout... | Changes the Slide Layout.

3 | Apply Design... | Changes the presentation design template.

OUTLINING TOOLBAR

The Outlining toolbar contains commands that edit and organize outlines.

1 Click the Promote/Demote icons to increase or decrease the indent of the selected paragraphs.

2 Click the Move Up or Move Down icons to move the selected slide or paragraphs up or down in the order.

3 Use the Collapse and Expand buttons to control how much of individual slides is seen.

4 Use the Collapse All button to see only titles of slides. Use the Show All button to see all of the text in a presentation.

5 Create a Summary slide with the title text of each slide in a presentation.

6 Use the Formatting button to toggle between showing the text with or without formatting.

ANIMATION EFFECTS

The Animation Effects toolbar contains commands to format builds and transitions.

1 Applies an animation effect to the text in the title placeholder.

2 Applies an animation effect to the text in the text placeholder.

3 Applies a Drive-In effect to the selected text or object.

4 Applies the Flying effect to the selected text or object.

5 Applies the Camera effect to the selected text or object.

6 Applies the Flash Once effect to the selected text or object.

7 Applies the Laser Title effect to the selected text or object.

8 Applies the Typewriter effect to the selected text or object.

9 Causes text to appear in reverse order, from bottom to top.

9 Causes text to appear in reverse order, from bottom to top.

10 Applies the Drop-in effect to the selected text or object.

11 Controls the order in which the objects are shown on a slide.

12 Opens the Custom Animation dialog box.

DRAWING TOOLBAR

The Drawing toolbar contains commands that help you to draw objects on a slide.

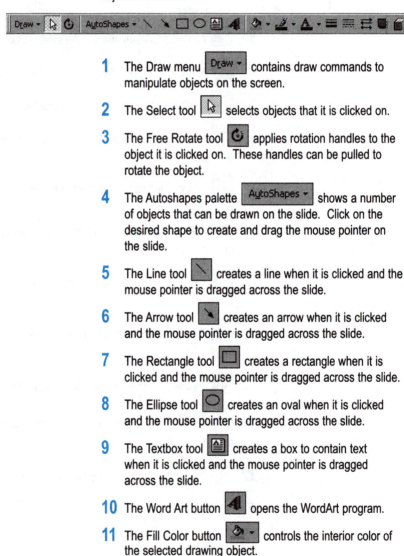

1 The Draw menu contains draw commands to manipulate objects on the screen.

2 The Select tool selects objects that it is clicked on.

3 The Free Rotate tool applies rotation handles to the object it is clicked on. These handles can be pulled to rotate the object.

4 The Autoshapes palette shows a number of objects that can be drawn on the slide. Click on the desired shape to create and drag the mouse pointer on the slide.

5 The Line tool creates a line when it is clicked and the mouse pointer is dragged across the slide.

6 The Arrow tool creates an arrow when it is clicked and the mouse pointer is dragged across the slide.

7 The Rectangle tool creates a rectangle when it is clicked and the mouse pointer is dragged across the slide.

8 The Ellipse tool creates an oval when it is clicked and the mouse pointer is dragged across the slide.

9 The Textbox tool creates a box to contain text when it is clicked and the mouse pointer is dragged across the slide.

10 The Word Art button opens the WordArt program.

11 The Fill Color button controls the interior color of the selected drawing object.

Notes:

- If you right-click on any toolbar, the toolbar menu appears.

12 The Line Color button ![Line Color icon] controls the outline color of the selected drawing object.

13 The Font Color button ![Font Color icon] sets the font color in a textbox.

14 The Line Style list ![Line Style icon] offers options as to line thickness.

15 The Dash Style list ![Dash Style icon] offers options as to line appearance.

16 The Arrow Style list ![Arrow Style icon] offers options as to arrow appearance.

17 The Shadow button ![Shadow icon] applies a shadow behind the selected drawing object.

18 The 3-D button ![3-D icon] makes the selected drawing object appear in 3-D.

SLIDE SORTER TOOLBAR

The Slide Sorter toolbar contains commands that affect how slides are presented during a slide show.

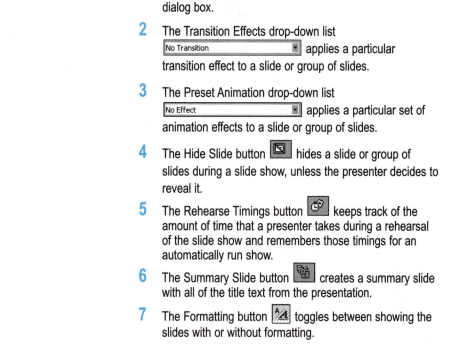

1 The Slide Transition button opens the Slide transition dialog box.

2 The Transition Effects drop-down list
No Transition applies a particular transition effect to a slide or group of slides.

3 The Preset Animation drop-down list
No Effect applies a particular set of animation effects to a slide or group of slides.

4 The Hide Slide button hides a slide or group of slides during a slide show, unless the presenter decides to reveal it.

5 The Rehearse Timings button keeps track of the amount of time that a presenter takes during a rehearsal of the slide show and remembers those timings for an automatically run show.

6 The Summary Slide button creates a summary slide with all of the title text from the presentation.

7 The Formatting button toggles between showing the slides with or without formatting.

Outlook

Microsoft Office's new scheduling and organization application. It provides you with a calendar, journal, contact list, task list and notes. Outlook also creates and manages e-mail, either through an online service or through a workplace network.
Outlook's components are fully integrated, so that you can send an e-mail scheduling a meeting, for example, and the appointment will automatically show up on your calendar.

Outlook is particularly useful in a networked environment, where it can serve to coordinate the activities of those who use it. It can be used to find mutually convenient times to schedule meetings, for instance, or to assign tasks to team members and track their progress.

Add an Event

An event is a special day that you wish to note on your calendar. Events do not affect the status of your time on the day of the event; you are still shown as Free. This procedure simply adds the name of an event to your calendar.

Calendar ➡ New Event

Notes:

- An event is attached to a particular day but not a time. For example, a holiday is an event. Like a holiday, the name of the event appears as a banner heading underneath the date heading.

1 Click **Calendar**, **New Event** in the Calendar window.

OR

Display the day of the event and double-click the date heading.

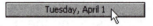

Tuesday, April 1

OR

Display the day of the event and type the event name (subject) under the date heading. Then double-click the event.

The Event dialog box appears.

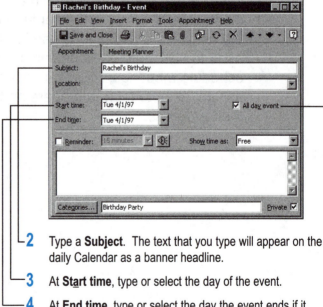

2 Type a **Subject**. The text that you type will appear on the daily Calendar as a banner headline.

3 At **Start time**, type or select the day of the event.

4 At **End time**, type or select the day the event ends if it spans more than one day.

> Note: For more ways to enter dates, see **Use AutoDate to Enter a Date or Time**. For example, using AutoDate you could type "for 4 days" and let Outlook calculate the end date.

5 Click **All day event** to select it, if necessary.

6   Enter any other information as desired.

7   Click ![Save and Close].

Edit an Event

1   Display the day on which the event appears.

2   Double-click the event banner to open the Event dialog box.

3   Set options as desired.

4   Click ![Save and Close].

Delete an Event

1   Display the date on which the event appears.

2   Click the banner under the date heading to select it.

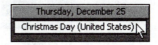

3   Click ☒.

Add Holidays to Your Calendar

Display holiday names in Day/Week/Month views. Holidays do not affect the status of your time; you are still shown as Free on that day. This procedure simply adds the names of holidays to your calendar.

Notes:

• If a holiday is a vacation day, follow **Edit an Event or Holiday** procedure and change the **Show time as** field to Out-of-Office.

1   Click **Tools**, **Options** to display the Options dialog box.

2   Click [Calendar] to display Calendar options.

3   Click [Add Holidays...] to display the Add Holidays dialog box.

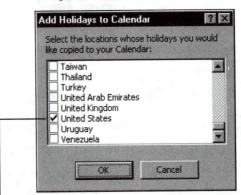

4   Click each country whose holidays you wish to add.

5   Click [OK].

Outlook imports the specified holiday file(s) and displays the Options dialog box.

6   Click [OK].

Edit a Holiday

1 Display the day on which the holiday appears.

2 Double-click the event banner to open the Event dialog box.

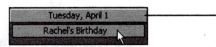

3 Set options as desired.

4 Click 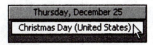.

Delete a Holiday

1 Display the date on which the holiday appears.

2 Click the banner under the date heading to select it.

> **Thursday, December 25**
> Christmas Day (United States)

3 Click ☒.

Create an Appointment

Use Calendar to maintain an appointment book and set visual and audio reminders to alert you before an appointment.

1 Click ⊞ or press **Ctrl+N** in the Calendar window.

OR

Display date and time of the appointment in the Calendar window. Double-click on the time. The date and time are filled in for you in the Appointment dialog box.

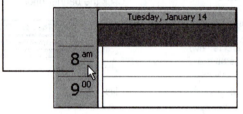

OR

Press **Ctrl+Shift+K** from anywhere in Outlook.

- To schedule entire days out of the office, such as vacation time, see **Schedule Out-of-Office Days**.

- If you schedule an appointment at the same time as an existing appointment, Outlook displays the message, "Conflicts with another appointment on your Calendar" in the Appointment dialog box.

- If you usually set a reminder, see the procedure called **Set Reminder Defaults** to set reminder options for the Appointment dialog box.

The Appointment dialog box appears.

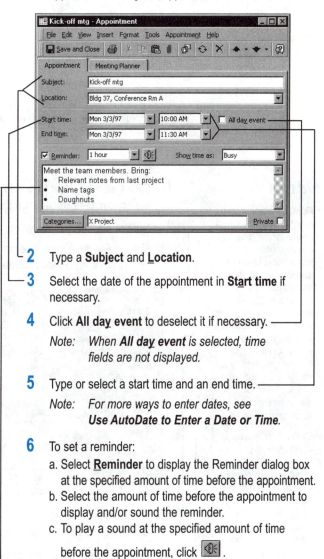

2 Type a **Subject** and **Location**.

3 Select the date of the appointment in **Start time** if necessary.

4 Click **All day event** to deselect it if necessary. ──────

Note: When **All day event** is selected, time fields are not displayed.

5 Type or select a start time and an end time. ──────

Note: For more ways to enter dates, see **Use AutoDate to Enter a Date or Time**.

6 To set a reminder:

a. Select **Reminder** to display the Reminder dialog box at the specified amount of time before the appointment.

b. Select the amount of time before the appointment to display and/or sound the reminder.

c. To play a sound at the specified amount of time before the appointment, click 📢.

7 Type notes in the text box.

Note: Click **Format** to change the font, align paragraphs, and add bullets in the text.

8 Click Categories... to assign one or more categories to the appointment.

9 Click 💾 Save and Close.

Create a Recurring Appointment

Schedule a series of appointments that occur on a regular basis. Recurring appointments are often meetings, such as a meeting held every Friday at 2 pm. Outlook creates each individual appointment within the series and adds them to your calendar.

Calendar ➡ 📅 New Recurring Appointment

Notes:

- Recurring appointments are most often meetings, unless you are responsible for scheduling meetings and inviting attendees. In that case, you would set up the recurring appointment as a meeting request. By using a meeting request rather than an appointment, you can use Outlook to quickly send out reminders or invitations to attendees.

- Creating a recurring appointment is similar to creating a regular appointment. The options are the same except that you enter recurrence pattern options when you create a recurring appointment.

1 Click **Calendar**, **New Recurring Appointment** to display the Appointment Recurrence dialog box.

2 Type or select the appointment **Start** time.

Note: *For more ways to enter dates, see*
Use AutoDate to Enter a Date or Time.

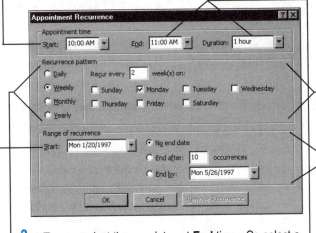

3 Type or select the appointment **End** time. Or, select a **Duration** and Outlook will calculate the end time for you.

4 Select a frequency for the recurring appointment.

Outlook displays Recurrence pattern options for the selected frequency.

5 Set Recurrence pattern options for selected frequency as desired.

Note: *Available options depend on the frequency selected.*

6 Type or select a **Start** date to specify the date of the first appointment in the series of recurring appointments.

7 Specify when the appointments should stop, if desired.

- You can edit a single instance of the recurring appointment if, for example, the meeting will be held in a different room on just one occasion. Or, change all appointments in the series if the meeting room is permanently changed.

8 Click [OK] to display the Appointment dialog box.

9 Set options as desired. See **Create an Appointment**. Fill in fields except for start and end times which are set in the Appointment Recurrence dialog box.

10 Click [🖫 Save and Close].

> — *Note:* *A recurrence symbol identifies recurring appointments in the Calendar window.*

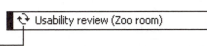

❘ ↻ Usability review (Zoo room)

Display a Second Time Zone

Display both the time in your time zone plus that in another time zone when working in Day view. For example, display a second time zone if you frequently call a contact in another time zone. The second time zone is visible only in Day view.

Notes:

Notes:

• You can switch Calendar over to a different time zone (**Swap Time Zones** in the Time Zone dialog box). Doing so changes the time zone in Windows Control Panel. All of your applications will use the new time.

1 Click **Tools**, **Options**.

2 Click [Calendar] to display Calendar options.

3 Click [Time Zone...] to display the Time Zone dialog box.

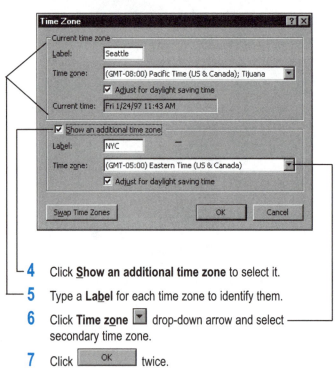

4 Click **Show an additional time zone** to select it.

5 Type a **Label** for each time zone to identify them.

6 Click **Time zone** [▼] drop-down arrow and select secondary time zone.

7 Click [OK] twice.

186

8 In Calendar, switch to Day view to display times in both zones.

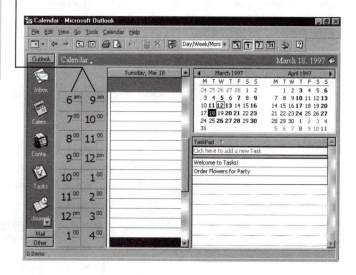

View Days, Weeks, or Months

Zoom in to view appointments for a single day in Day view. Or, display your appointments for a week in Week view or an entire month in Month view. You can easily switch between views.

1 Click **Current View** drop-down arrow to open the list of views. Select Day/Week/Month.

2 To switch between the different views in Day/Week/Month view:

- Click **Day** [1] or press **Alt+1** to switch to Day view.
- Click **Week** [7] or press **Alt+–** to switch to Week view.
- Click **Month** [31] or press **Alt+=** to switch to Month view.

Hide Outlook Bar

Make more room on your screen for appointments by removing the Outlook Bar from the Calendar window. To redisplay the Outlook Bar, repeat the procedure.

Select **View**, **Outlook Bar**.

> *Note: Repeat to show the Outlook Bar.*

Display (Go To) Current Day

Click **Go to Today** [icon].

Display (Go To) Any Day

1 Press **Ctrl+G** to display the Go To Date dialog box.

Type date to go to in **Date** text box.

OR

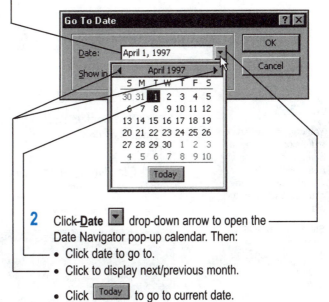

2 Click **Date** ▼ drop-down arrow to open the Date Navigator pop-up calendar. Then:

• Click date to go to.

• Click to display next/previous month.

• Click Today to go to current date.

Move Between Appointments in Day View

• Press **Tab** to go to the next appointment

• Press **Shift+Tab** to go to the previous appointment.

• Press the **right arrow** key to go the next day.

• Press the **left arrow** key to go to the previous day.

Add a Contact

Enter address, phone number, e-mail address, and other information about one person. If you include a fax number or e-mail address, Outlook adds the contact to the Outlook Address Book. You can use the address book to send mail to contacts using Outlook Mail and send faxes using Microsoft Fax.

Notes:

- You can include an extension in a phone number, for example: 555-5555 x439. Outlook ignores the extension when auto-dialing.

- Start international phone numbers with the country code.

1 Click **New Contact** or press **Ctrl+N** from the Contacts window.

OR

Click **File**, **New**, **Contact** or press **Ctrl+Shift+C** from anywhere in Outlook.

The Contact dialog box appears.

2 Enter contact information in the Contact dialog box. Most fields are self-explanatory. Here are some tips:

- Select the name under which to file the contact in **File As**. Outlook files contacts by this information so what you select here determines the letter under which the contact will be stored.

- Click drop-down arrow under the Address button and select an address type to enter up to three addresses.

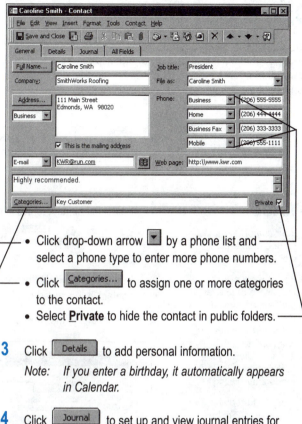

• Click drop-down arrow 🔽 by a phone list and select a phone type to enter more phone numbers.

• Click **Categories...** to assign one or more categories to the contact.

• Select **Private** to hide the contact in public folders.

3 Click **Details** to add personal information.

Note: If you enter a birthday, it automatically appears in Calendar.

4 Click **Journal** to set up and view journal entries for the contact.

5 Click **💾 Save and Close** to save the contact and return to the Contacts window.

OR

Click **Save and New** 📧 to save the contact and add another contact.

OR

Click **File**, **Save and New in Company** to save the contact and add a new contact using the same address and phone number as the current contact.

Dial a Contact

Use AutoDial to have Outlook dial the phone number of a contact for you. Outlook can automatically create a journal entry to record information about the phone call. Information such as the contact name and the length of the call are recorded in the journal entry.

Notes:

- Your computer must have a modem to dial from Outlook.

- If you use a switching device to use fax, modem, and voice mail on one line, this procedure will not work unless the switcher allows you to switch to voice mode after dialing.

- You can autodial phone numbers in the speed dial list from anywhere in Outlook. To dial other numbers, you must be in Contacts.

1 Select the contact to call in the Contacts window.

Click **AutoDialer** in the toolbar.

OR

Press **Ctrl+Shift+D** from anywhere in Outlook to call a contact in the speed dial list.

2 Set options in the New Call dialog box as desired.

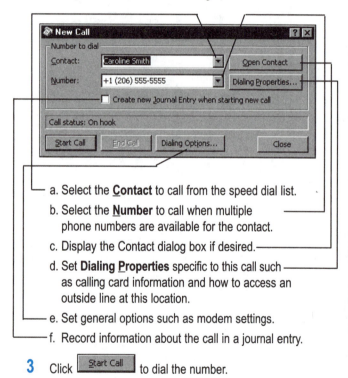

a. Select the **Contact** to call from the speed dial list.

b. Select the **Number** to call when multiple phone numbers are available for the contact.

c. Display the Contact dialog box if desired.

d. Set **Dialing Properties** specific to this call such as calling card information and how to access an outside line at this location.

e. Set general options such as modem settings.

f. Record information about the call in a journal entry.

3 Click Start Call to dial the number.

4 Pick up the phone receiver. Then click Talk.

Notes:

- At any time, you can disconnect by clicking

  [Hang **U**p]
  .

- If creating a journal entry, Outlook starts the timer after dialing. You can stop the clock at any time by clicking

  [Pa**u**se Timer]
  .

  To resume, click

  [Start Ti**m**er]
  .

Notes:

- Outlook stores the phone numbers that you last autodialed even after you exit Outlook. Select a phone number from a list of recently-dialed numbers when using Outlook to dial a contact. You can redial from anywhere in Outlook; you do not have to return to the Contacts window.

5 When finished with the call, hang up the phone.

6 Click in the Windows taskbar to display the New Call dialog box.

7 Click [End Call] to stop the timer.

8 If Outlook created a journal entry for the call, click [**S**ave and Close] in the journal entry.

Redial a Contact

1 Click **Tools**, **D**ial, **R**edial.

2 Select number to dial.

3 Follow **Dial a Contact** procedure from step 3

193

Create and Send a Mail Message

Create a new mail message. Use your Address Book to select one or more recipients. Then, send the message.

Notes:

- If you are working offline, the message is stored in the Outbox until you send all messages.

1 Click **New Mail Message** 📧 or press **Ctrl+N** from the Mail window.

OR

Click **File**, **New**, **Mail Message** or press **Ctrl+Shift+M** from anywhere in Outlook.

The Message dialog box appears.

2 Click ☐ To... to open the Select Names dialog box to select recipients from an address book.

Note: You can type rather than select recipient names. Skip to step 4.

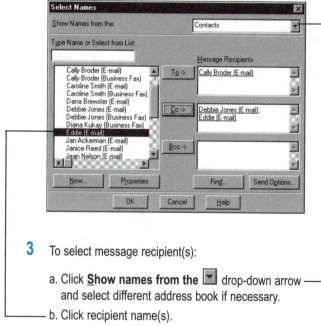

3 To select message recipient(s):

a. Click **Show names from the** 🔽 drop-down arrow and select different address book if necessary.

b. Click recipient name(s).

*Note: To select multiple names, press **Ctrl** and click next name.*

c. Click 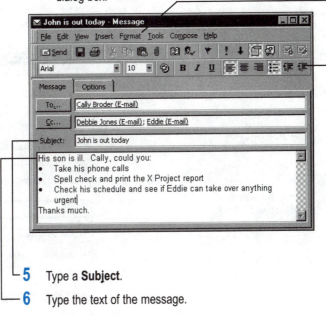 To -> to add selected names as recipients.

OR

Click Cc -> to add selected names as Carbon Copy recipients

OR

Click Bcc -> to add selected names as Blind Carbon Copy recipients.

d. Repeat from step a to add more recipients if desired.

e. Click OK . Outlook displays the Message dialog box.

5 Type a **Subject**.

6 Type the text of the message.

7 Click formatting buttons or **Format** menu to format message text if desired.

8 Click Send to send the message.

195

Flag a Message

Add a flag to mark messages that require follow-up. You can flag messages that you send and messages in your Inbox. You can also specify a due date for the follow-up action.

Notes:

- Set a flag type and also a due date if desired. For example, you could set a Review flag and specify that the review is due June 5.

- If you specify a due date with a flag, Outlook displays the Reminder dialog box at the specified date and time.

- The flag appears in the message list in the Mail window.

1 Display message to flag.

2 Click ⬇ to display the Flag Message dialog box.

3 Click the **Flag** ⬇ drop-down arrow and select flag type.

4 Click the **By** ⬇ drop-down arrow and select a due date if desired.

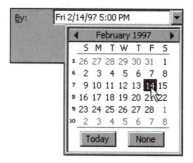

5 Click ⬛ OK ⬛.

Format the Current View

Change the font, table gridlines, and other settings.

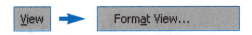

View ➡ Format View...

Notes:

- In addition to the Format View dialog box, you can customize a view using other commands on the View menu. Available options on the menu depend on whether the view that you are customizing is a Table view or a Timeline view. For example, in a Table view, the View menu includes the Format Columns command for setting up columns in the table.

1 Click **View**, **Format View** to display the Format View dialog box.

Note: Options on the Format View dialog box vary depending on whether the current view is in a Timeline view or a Table view. The following illustration shows options for a Table view.

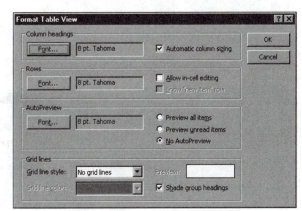

2 Set options as desired.

3 Click [OK].

Format Your Comments in Messages that You Forward or Reply to

Set up default formatting for text that you add to messages that you forward and messages that you reply to. You normally format your comments in order to distinguish them from the comments of others who contribute to a message.

Notes:

- If you use Word as your default e-mail editor (**Tools**, **Options**, **E-mail** tab), some of these options, such as font options, are not available.

- When you set up your own formatting for messages that you reply to, your comments will be easy to distinguish from other people's comments who are also sending replies to the original message.

- When you set up your own formatting for messages that you forward, your comments will be easy to distinguish from the text of the forwarded message.

1 Click **Tools**, **Options** from anywhere in Outlook to display the Options dialog box.

2 Click ⬚ Reading ⬚.

3 Select formatting options for text that you type when replying to messages:

- Click ▾ drop-down arrow to open a list of options for including the text of the original message.

- Click ⬚ Font... ⬚ to open the Font dialog box. You can format your comments in a different font, font size, and color.

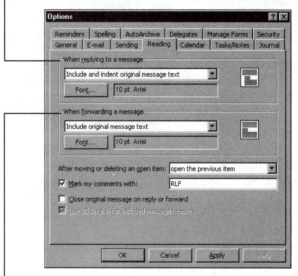

4 Select formatting options for text that you type when forwarding messages:

- Click ▾ drop-down arrow to open a list of options for formatting the text of the original message that you are forwarding.

- Click ▾ to open the Font dialog box. You can format your comments in a different font, font size, and color.

5 Click **After moving or deleting an open item** drop-down arrow to specify what you want to happen after you move or delete an open mail message.

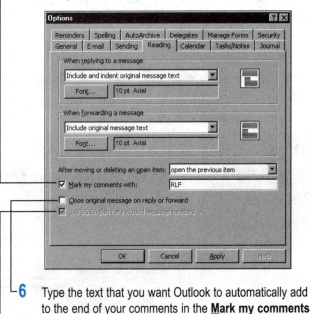

6 Type the text that you want Outlook to automatically add to the end of your comments in the **Mark my comments with**: text box.

7 Click **Close original message on reply or forward** if you want to automatically close the message that you are forwarding or replying to.

Note: Outlook creates a new mail message when you reply to or forward a message. This option sets whether or not the original message should also remain open on the screen.

8 Click OK .

Reply to a Mail Message

When you receive a mail message, you can respond to it directly from the message. Send your response to the person who wrote the original mail message or send it to all recipients of the original message.

Notes:

- Use the **Reading** tab options on the **Tools**, **Options** menu to set the default formatting of all your replies.

1 Open message to respond to.

2 Click [Reply] or press **Ctrl+R** to reply to the person who sent the mail.

OR

Click [Reply to All] or press **Ctrl+Shift+R** to reply to the sender and all recipients (listed in the Cc: and Bcc: fields) of the original mail message.

3 Type message in text box.

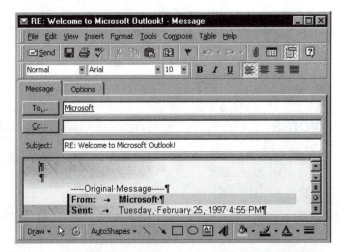

4 Click .

Set an AutoSignature

An AutoSignature is your personal signature. You can have Outlook automatically add your AutoSignature to mail that you send. You can create an AutoSignature in Outlook or in a graphics program.

Notes:

- Personalize your mail messages with a custom AutoSignature. You can have Outlook automatically add your AutoSignature to your mail messages or you can insert it in individual messages.

- Use this procedure to create your AutoSignature using fonts available in the AutoSignature dialog box. You can also create an AutoSignature in another program, such as a graphics program, and copy and paste it into the dialog box.

1 Create a new mail message that contains the signature you want to have as your AutoSignature. Select the signature and then click **Tools**, **AutoSignature** from the Message menu.

OR

Click **Tools**, **AutoSignature** from Mail to display the AutoSignature dialog box.

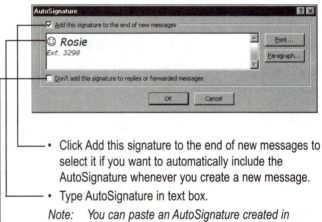

- Click Add this signature to the end of new messages to select it if you want to automatically include the AutoSignature whenever you create a new message.

- Type AutoSignature in text box.

Note: *You can paste an AutoSignature created in another program, such as a graphics program. Copy the graphic, switch to the AutoSignature dialog box, then press **Ctrl+V**.*

2 Click ⬚Font...⬚ to format the font of selected text, if desired.

3 Click ⬚Paragraph...⬚ to align selected paragraph(s) and/or add bullets, if desired.

4 Select **Don't add this signature to replies or forwarded messages** to omit the AutoSignature when you reply to or forward a mail message.

5 Click ⬚OK⬚.

Note: *To insert an AutoSignature in a mail message, position cursor in message text box and click **Insert**, **AutoSignature**.*

Set the Default Address Book

When you create a mail message, you can open the Address Book dialog box to select recipients. The dialog box can display names from only one address book at a time. Use this procedure to set which address book is opened automatically when you display the dialog box.

Notes:

- This procedure sets the address book that appears first in the Address Book dialog box. You can open a different address book in the dialog box.

1 Click **Tools**, **Services** to display the Services dialog box.

2 Click Addressing to display addressing options.

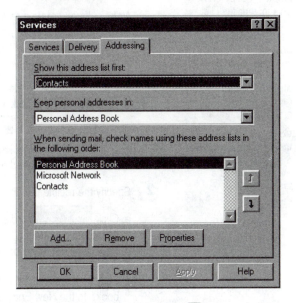

3 Click **Show this address list first** drop-down arrow to display available address books.

4 Select the address book that you want to appear whenever you open the Address Book.

5 Click OK.

Assign a Task (Send a Task Request)

Transfer ownership and responsibility for a task to someone else by sending a task request. A task request is a kind of mail message. If you are a project manager, create all tasks for a project and then assign each individual task to a member of your team.

Notes:

- Assigning a task creates a copy of the task in your task list so that you can keep track of all tasks in a project, even those assigned to someone else. You can receive automatic status reports and updates on assigned tasks.

- When you assign a task, Outlook creates a special type of mail message called a task request.

1 Press **Ctrl+N** to open the Task dialog box to create a new task if necessary. See **Create a Task** for help on setting options.

Note: If you create a task using this method, the Task dialog box does not include an Owner field. The Owner field will automatically be set to the recipient when you send the task request.

OR

Double-click existing task in task list to open it.

Then click **Assign Task** 🗹.

Note: The Owner field will be changed to the recipient when you send the task request.

2 Specify the recipient of the task request:

a. Click [To...] to display the Select Task Recipient dialog box.

b. Type recipient name or select from list.

c. Select [New...] if the recipient is not in an address book. In the New Entry dialog box, either add the recipient to an address book or use the address temporarily to send the task request. Then click [OK] to return to the Select Task Recipient dialog box.

d. Click [To...] to use the specified name as the recipient.

e. Click [OK] to return to the Task dialog box.

- When the recipient receives the task request, they can accept, decline, or assign the task to someone else.

3 Select or deselect **Keep an updated copy of this task on my task list**. If selected, every time the owner changes the task, your copy of the task is updated with the change.

4 Select or deselect **Send me a status report when this task is complete**. If selected, Outlook automatically sends you a status report when the owner marks the task as completed.

5 Click [Send] or press **Ctrl+Enter** to send the task request.

Outlook sends the message and displays a message in the Task dialog box for the task: "Waiting for response from recipient" to remind you that the task has not yet been accepted by the contact. The Owner field is changed to name of the recipient of the task request.

Create a Recurring Task

A recurring task is a series of repeating tasks. Examples of recurring tasks might be submitting a status report every two weeks or calling a contact every six months. You need only create a single recurring task and Outlook will take care of creating tasks in the series on an ongoing basis.

Notes:

Outlook creates two types of recurring tasks:

1. Recurring tasks based on a pattern of specific dates such as every other Friday or the third Saturday of each month. When a recurring task falls due, Outlook calculates the next due date and creates the next recurring task.

2. Recurring tasks that depend on the completion of the previous task. Outlook creates the next recurring task when you mark the current task as complete. The date on which you mark the task as complete is the date used to calculate the next due date. For example, if you call a particular client every three months, you don't want to schedule the next call until you actually contact the client.

1 Click **New Task** ☑ or press **Ctrl+N** from the Task window to display the Task dialog box.

2 Type a **Subject** for the task. The subject appears as the title in the task list.

3 Click **Recurrence** ↻ to display the Task Recurrence dialog box.

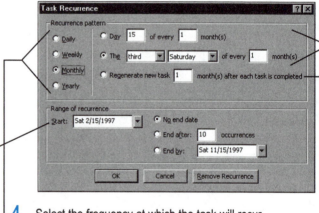

4 Select the frequency at which the task will recur.

5 Specify the kind of recurring task to create:

Click **Regenerate new task** to create a recurrence pattern dependent on the completion of the task. Outlook creates the first recurring task using the due date that you provide. OR

Set options for selected frequency to automatically create a new task at the specified time interval.

Note: Recurrence pattern options vary depending on selected frequency.

6 Type a **Start** date or click ▼ to select from pop-up calendar.

*Note: Outlook creates the first in the series of recurring tasks on the specified **Start** date.*

7 Select a date at which Outlook will stop creating recurring tasks if desired.

Note: *If **Regenerate new task** is selected, you cannot set an **End by** date.*

8 Click [OK] to return to the Task dialog box.

Note: *In the Task dialog box, the **Due** date is set to the next occurrence of the task.*

9 Set other fields in the Task dialog box if desired. See **Create a Task**.

Note: *Do not change date fields, as these are set up according to the recurrence pattern.*

10 Click [Save and Close] .

Skip a Recurring Task

Sometimes you need to skip an individual task in a series of recurring tasks. For example, your recurring task is to write a monthly newsletter article, but the newsletter is not published in the month of January. So, you skip the task scheduled for January.

1 Open the recurring task.

2 Click T**a**sk, S**k**ip Occurrence.

3 Click [Save and Close] .

Create a Task

A task is a single action item that must be completed either by a particular due date or an unspecified time. Create a task for each action item. Then you can track the progress of a task until its completion.

Notes:

- Tasks are also visible in the TaskPad in Calendar.

- Tasks that are past due (not marked complete on the due date) appear in red in the task list.

- You can have Outlook display a reminder at a specified date and time.

- To enter a date by typing text such as "2 weeks from today" see **Use AutoDate to Enter a Date or Time** in the chapter on **Calendar**.

1 Click **New Task** [▣] or press **Ctrl+N** in the Task window.

OR

Click **File, New, Task** or press **Ctrl+Shift+K** from anywhere in Outlook.

The Task dialog box appears.

2 Type a description in **Subject**.

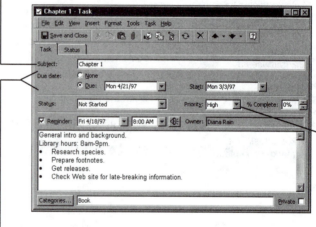

3 Specify a due date:

- Select **None** if the task is not due on a specific date.

- Type a **Due** date or click [▼] to select from pop-up calendar.

- Type a **Start** date or click [▼] to select from pop-up calendar.

4 Select High, Normal, or Low **Priority**.

Note: *High priority tasks appear with a red exclamation point in the task list.*

5 Set reminder options:
- Click **Reminder** to select or deselect. If selected, Reminder dialog box displays at the specified date and time.
- Select date and time to display and/or sound the reminder.
- Click 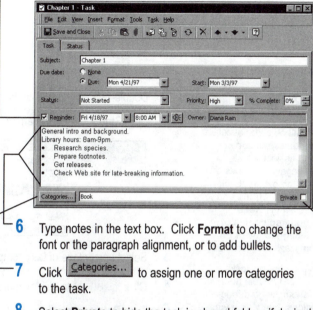 to enable or disable the reminder sound.

6 Type notes in the text box. Click **Format** to change the font or the paragraph alignment, or to add bullets.

7 Click **Categories...** to assign one or more categories to the task.

8 Select **Private** to hide the task in shared folders if desired.

9 Click **Status** to display more options.

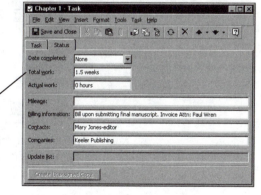

10 Type number of hours, days, or weeks task is expected to take in **Total work**. Outlook changes hours to days or weeks.

11 Type mileage, billing, contact, and company information if desired.

12 Click **Save and Close**.

Update Task Status

Keep track of the progress you have made on a task. Once you start a task, set the status to In Progress. Every time you work on a task, update the number of hours that you have spent on it.

1 Double-click on the task in the task list to open it.

2 Click **Status** drop-down arrow ▼ to select a new status.

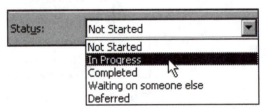

3 Select percentage of task completed at % Complete.

4 Click [Status] to display more options.

5 Type **Date completed** or click drop-down arrow ▼ to select completion date if the task is finished.

*Note: If you use **Complete a Task** procedure, Outlook automatically fills in the completion date as the current date.*

6 Type the number of hours, days, or weeks devoted to the task at **Actual work**. Use this field to keep an ongoing record of time spent on the task.

7 Click [💾 Save and Close].

Notes:

- You can have Outlook automatically send you a status report when tasks that you have assigned are completed. Click **Tools**, **Options** and select the **Send status reports when assigned tasks are completed** check box.

Notes:

- You can archive tasks before you delete them if you think that you might need to refer to them in the future.

- Use this procedure to delete a single recurring task or all tasks in the series.

Mark a Task as Complete

When you have finished a task, mark it as complete. This does not delete the task. Completed tasks appear dimmed and crossed out in the task list.

1   Double-click the task icon in the task list to open Task dialog box.

2   Click **Mark Complete** 🖉 .

Delete a Task

Remove a task from the task list. Deleted tasks are moved to Deleted Items where you can retrieve them until they are permanently deleted.

1   Click the task icon in the task list to select the task.

2   Click ☒ or press **Ctrl+D**.

Note: *If you are deleting a recurring task, Outlook displays a prompt asking you if you want to delete only the current task or the entire series of recurring tasks.*

Integration

Each of the Office tools can be used separately, or they can be used together to produce professional looking documents. For example, a report done in Word can be enhanced with charts and graphs created in Excel or slides created in PowerPoint. Because Microsoft Office is designed to have all the components working together, integrating the separate applications can be easily done.

Windowing Files from Different Applications

Microsoft Office allows you to work with several files simultaneously–the files can all be from the same application or they can be from different applications. For example, you can move between an opened Word document and an Excel workbook.

1 To minimize a window, click the minimize button on the upper-right hand corner of the Menu bar.

2 The minimized file will be become a button on the taskbar at the bottom of the screen.

3 By clicking on the button, you can access the open file in the program that it was created in.

OR

If you wish to view the files from several programs at the same time:

1 Right-click on the Taskbar on the bottom of your screen;

2 Select the view option you prefer. You may **Cascade, Tile Horizontally**, or **Tile Vertically.**

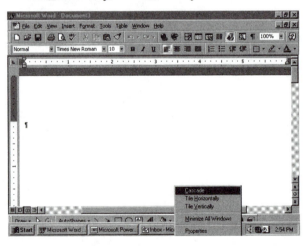

Note: If you are copying sections from a document in one application to a document in another application, cascading your files is a convenient way to work.

Export an Access Database to an Excel File

You may wish to use an Excel workbook to summarize and analyze information saved in an Access database. This can be accomplished by exporting, or sending, data from Access to Excel.

Notes:

- Exporting is used if you wish to create a new workbook file with the database of with part of a database table.

- By selecting **Tools**, **Office Links**, you can automatically bring an Access database into Excel or Word. However, by using this quick feature you have no control over selecting options.

1 Open the Access file that you want to export.

2 Select (highlight) the table.

3 Click **Save As/Export** from the **File** menu.

4 The **Save As** dialog box opens. If **To an External File or Database** is not selected, click to select it.

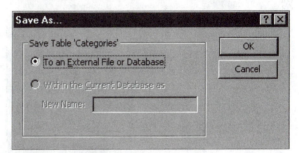

5 The **Save Table 'filename' In** dialog box opens.

- Type a file name in the File name dialog box.
- Select Microsoft Excel 97 form the **Save as type** drop-down list.
- Select the **Save Formatted** check box to preserve data formats.
- Click **Export**.

6 Close the Access file, and then switch to Excel to open the new file.

Export a PowerPoint Presentation into a Word Document

You can include a complete PowerPoint presentation in a Word document so that the slides may be viewed one at a time.

Notes:

• If you wish to bring only one slide into a Word document, you can use the **Copy**, **Paste Special**, **Paste** link procedure. When you use this procedure, the data will be linked.

1 Open the PowerPoint Presentation that you wish to export into Word.

2 Select **Send To**, **Microsoft Word** from the **File** menu.

3 Select the desired layout option from the **Write-Up** dialog box.

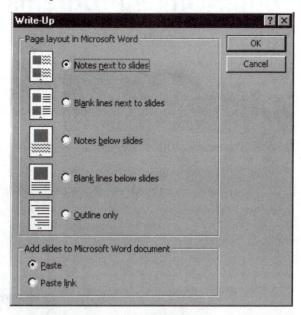

4 If desired, select the **Paste link** option. If this option is selected, then you can double-click on the PowerPoint object in Word and PowerPoint toolbars and menus will become visible.

5 Click [OK].

Export Information from Outlook to other Office Programs

This procedure allows you to export Outlook files for use in another application.

Notes:

• If you export to a file for use in Word or PowerPoint, choose either the Tab Separated Values or the Comma Separated Values field types from the Create a file of type options.

1 Click **Import and Export** form the **File** Menu.

2 Click **Export to a file** from the **Choose an action to perform list**, and then click Next >.

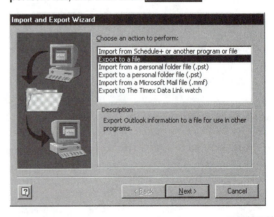

3 **Select folder to export from**, and then click Next >.

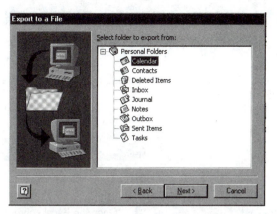

4   Select what type of file you wish to create, and then click
    Next > .

5   Type name of what you want to **Save exported file as** or
    click Browse... . Then, click Next > .

6   The Export to a File dialog box appears noting the action
    that you are about to perform. Click Finish to begin
    the export procedure.

Integrate an Excel Worksheet File and a Word Document

An Excel chart or worksheet can add supporting or visual documentation to a Word document.

Notes:

- The File that you are taking the data from is called the **source file** and the file that is receiving the data is the **destination file**. For example, if you are integrating an Excel chart into a report that was created in Word, the Excel file would be the source file and the Word file would be the destination file.

1 Open the Excel source file.

2 Highlight the worksheet or chart area that you wish to copy.

3 Click **Edit**, **Copy** or **Ctrl+C**.

4 Open the Word file (destination file) and place your insertion point at the location where you wish to insert the source file.

5 Click **Edit**, **Paste Special**.

The Paste Special Dialog Box appears.

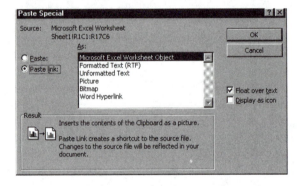

6 Select **Microsoft Excel Worksheet Object** in the **As** list box.

7 If desired, click **Paste link**. If this option is selected, the object in the destination file will be automatically updated if any edits or changes are made to the source file.

8 Click [OK].

*Note: Using the **Paste**, **Paste Special** procedure allows you to make edits to the chart or worksheet in Word without changing the source material. When the chart is double-clicked, Excel menus and toolbars appear. You can then return to the Word document by clicking outside the Excel object.*

Index

Basics

Word

A

B

C

D

E

F

G

PowerPoint

Outlook

Integration

 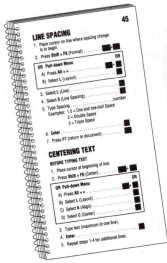

Short Course Learning Books
Approximately 25 hours of instruction per book

We sliced our learning books into short courses, *introductory & intermediate*.

- We extracted pages from our Fast-teach Learning books and created shortened versions.
- Each book comes with a data disk to eliminate typing the exercise.

Title	Cat. No.	Title	Cat. No.	Title	Cat. No.
Access 2 Introductory	AB-10	Microsoft Office 4.3 Introductory	AB-14	WordPerfect 6.1 Win Introductory	AB-1
Access 7 Introductory	AB-23	Microsoft Office Win 95 Introductory	AB-15	WordPerfect 6.1 Win Intermediate	AB-2
DOS Introductory	AB-13	PowerPoint 4 Introductory	AB-11	Word 6 Windows Introductory	AB-4
Excel 5 Windows Introductory	AB-7	PowerPoint 7 Introductory	AB-24	Word 6 Windows Intermediate	AB-5
Excel 5 Windows Intermediate	AB-8	Windows 3.1 Introductory	AB-12	Word 7 Windows 95 Introductory	AB-17
Excel 7 Windows 95 Introductory	AB-20				

New Short Courses (College Level)....$25ea.
Teacher Manual and Exercise Solutions on Diskette ....$12ea.
Files saved in Word 7

Title	Cat No.
Microsoft Office Windows 95	AB-15
Pagemaker 6 Intro	AB-16
No Teacher Manual	
Word 7 Intro	AB-17
Word 7 Intermediate	AB-18
Word 7 Advanced	AB-19
Excel 7 Intro	AB-20
Excel 7 Intermediate	AB-21
PowerPoint 7 Intro	AB-15
Access 7 Intro	AB-23

DDC Publishing 275 Madison Avenue, New York, NY 10016

----- ORDER FORM -----

QTY.	CAT. NO.	DESCRIPTION

Check enclosed. Add $2.50 for postage & handling & $1 postage for each additional guide. NY State residents add local sales tax.

Visa   Mastercard   ***100% Refund Guarantee***

No._____ Exp._____

Name_____

Firm _____

Address_____

City, State, Zip _____

Phone (800) 528-3897   Fax (800) 528-3862

(DDC) *Computer based training puts an interactive teacher in your computer*

For Microsoft® Office Windows® 95 to teach Word 7, Excel 7, Access 7, and PowerPoint 7

You hear, you see, you do, you learn.

Our teachers present instructions to you orally and visually live and on screen. Our Multimedia CD ROM takes the written word off the page, explains the concept, and tells you what to do. This teacher sits at your elbow, sight unseen, ready to correct your errors and tell you how to do it, until you get it correct.

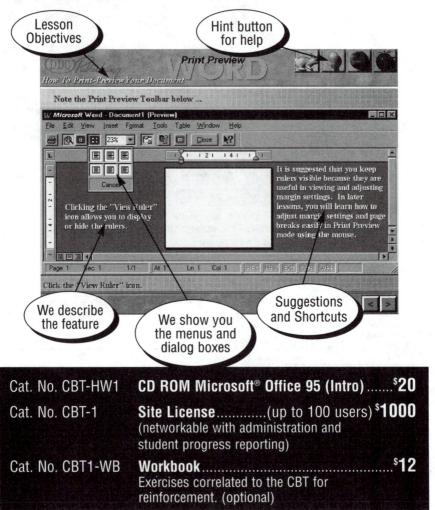

To Order - Phone: 800-528-3897 Fax: 800-528-3862

More Fast-teach Learning Books

Did we make one for you?

Title	Cat. No.
Corel WordPerfect 7 for Win 95	Z12
DOS 5–6.2 (Book & Disk)	D9
DOS + Windows	Z7
Excel 5 for Windows	E9
Excel 7 for Windows 95	XL7
INTERNET	Z15
Lotus 1-2-3 Rel. 2.2–4.0 for DOS	L9
Lotus 1-2-3 Rel. 4 & 5 for Windows	B9
Microsoft Office	M9
Microsoft Office for Windows 95	Z6
Windows 3.1 – A Quick Study	WQS-1
Windows 95	Z3
Word 2 for Windows	K9
Word 6 for Windows	1-WDW6
Word 7 for Windows 95	Z10
WordPerfect 5.0 & 5.1 for DOS	W9
WordPerfect 6 for DOS	P9
WordPerfect 6 for Windows	Z9
WordPerfect 6.1 for Windows	H9
Works 3 for Windows	1-WKW3
Works 4 for Windows 95	Z8

DESKTOP PUBLISHING LEARNING BOOKS	
Word 6 for Windows	Z2
WordPerfect 5.1 for DOS	WDB
WordPerfect 6 for Windows	F9
WordPerfect 6.1 for Windows	Z5

Learning The Internet

What we teach:

- Searching Techniques

- Browsers/Search Engines
  -MS Explorer
  -Netscape
  -Yahoo
  -Web Crawler

- Sources of Information
  -Telnet
  -Usenet
  -E-mail
  -WWW Virtual Library
  -Electronic Encyclopedias
  -CD-ROM

- Using the Information

  -Notepad

  -Word Processors

  -Compiling

  -Download Utilities

Cat. No. Z-15 ISBN 1-56243-345-8

Learning the Internet......$27

Learning the Internet Simulation CD-ROM

- Now you don't need to connect to the Web to teach Internet concepts.

- Simulates the sites and hyperlinks used in DDC's *Learning the Internet* book.

Cat. No. Z-15CD..........$20

275 Madison Avenue,
New York, NY 10016

FREE CATALOG
AND
UPDATED LISTING

We don't just have books that find
your answers faster; we also have
books that teach you how to use
your computer without the fairy
tales and the gobbledygook.

We also have books to improve
your typing, spelling
and punctuation.

**Return this card for a free
catalog and mailing list update.**

DDC *Publishing*

275 Madison Avenue,
New York, NY 10016

☐ Please send me your catalog
and put me on your mailing list.

Name

Firm (if any)

Address

City, State, Zip

Phone (800) 528-3897   Fax (800) 528-3862

**SEE OUR COMPLETE CATALOG ON THE
INTERNET @: http://www.ddcpub.com**